KARA

KARA

SHARON DAVIS MESSER

REVIEW AND HERALD® PUBLISHING ASSOCIATION
WASHINGTON, DC 20039-0555
HAGERSTOWN, MD 21740

Copyright © 1989 by
Review and Herald® Publishing Association

This book was
Edited by Gerald Wheeler
Designed by Bill Kirstein
Cover illustration by Peter Fiore

Printed in U.S.A.

Texts credited to NIV are from the
Holy Bible, New International Version.
Copyright © 1973, 1978, International Bible Society.
Used by permission of
Zondervan Bible Publishers.

R&H Cataloging Service
Messer, Sharon M   Davis, 1953-
  Kara.

  1. Missionaries, Student—Marshall Islands.
I. Title.

        266.679

ISBN 0-8280-0487-0

THIS BOOK IS
LOVINGLY DEDICATED

to my husband, Gary
to Jon, Sherlyn, and Donnell
and to
all those who have gone and who
will go as student missionaries
to
the Marshall Islands

Contents

1. Here Goes — 9
2. Lizard Soup, Anyone? — 16
3. On Strike — 24
4. The Stranger — 32
5. Mr. Know-It-All — 42
6. "Help! I Can't Swim!" — 48
7. Ronn to the Rescue — 54
8. Typhoon! — 61
9. The Christmas Ride — 66
10. The White Foreigner — 72
11. Troubles — 77
12. The Argument — 85
13. The Sign of Mourning — 90
14. Tomfooler Rides Again — 96
15. When You Leave He Will Cry — 104
16. Midnight Swim — 110
17. Good-bye, Tomfooler, Good-bye — 116

Here Goes

1

"Frontier Flight 62 is now ready for boarding. Will all passengers bound for Denver, Salt Lake City, and San Francisco proceed to boarding gate number two. All passengers boarding Frontier . . ."

"Oh! That's for me!" Kara's heart skipped an extra beat as sudden panic swept through her.

Paul put his arms around her. "I'll sure miss you, Kara."

"And I'll miss you. Seems like forever until we'll be together again."

"Any amount of time seems like forever when you're not with me."

The tall brown-headed girl felt like swooning. "You'll write often, won't you?"

He chuckled and his brown eyes twinkled merrily as he teased, "I'll write so often that the post office will have to add on another room just to handle my letters."

She managed to giggle nervously. Turning, she hugged her big sister. Tears sprang to Kara's eyes as she heard Kathryn say wistfully, "If only Mom would have lived to see this day. She would have been so proud!" Then her mothering instincts took over as she asked, "Now, you're sure you have everything? You didn't forget your visa? Money? Toothpaste? Oh, no, I think you did. I saw it . . ."

KARA

The intercom interrupted. "Last call for Flight 62 . . ."

Grabbing her things, Kara hastily assured her sister, "Don't worry, I'll buy more paste." Before picking up her accordion she hugged her boyfriend one last time.

Placing a lingering kiss on her lips in spite of onlookers, Paul whispered, "I love you!"

She tried to reply but the words seemed to stick in her throat. Glancing at the boarding gate, Kara realized she'd better hurry. "Gotta go. Bye! See you in ten months!" As she spoke, she gathered her paraphernalia and walked awkwardly to the gate. A quick turn and she waved one last time.

Once on the aircraft she took a window seat near the front. The stewardess helped stash her bags. As Kara glanced out the tiny window, last minute jitters seized her. Ten months suddenly seemed like forever. When she had applied for a student missionary position there had been no boyfriend to complicate the picture. "Is it worth being separated from Paul for almost a year? What if he finds a new girlfriend at college while I'm so far away?" She frowned in consternation.

"I'm sure to get homesick. Then what? And that ocean. I can't swim! Why am I going to . . . to . . . an island?" Her eyes widened as she gulped, "Sharks. There's sure to be sharks . . ."

Sucking in a deep breath, Kara squeezed her eyes tightly shut and prayed. "Lord, You said You'd go with me . . . even unto the ends of the earth . . . and that's where I'm going . . . and I'm scared . . . so please give me the courage to be the kind of missionary You'd

HERE GOES

have me to be. And about Paul. Please don't let distance separate our love for each other."

"Mind if I sit here?"

Startled, she glanced up to see a white-haired woman gazing pleasantly down at her. "No. Not at all."

Once airborne, the woman asked, "Where are you going, dear?"

"To the Marshall Islands." Then she hastened to add, "They're in the middle of the Pacific, midway between Hawaii and Australia."

"Whatever for?"

"I'm going as a student missionary to teach in an elementary school. There'll be one other teacher, Lynn. She'll meet me in San Francisco."

Seeing her confusion, Kara explained, "I haven't graduated from college yet. I just finished my sophomore year, but my church, that is, the Seventh-day Adventist Church, has a program that enables students to take a year out of their studies to go as volunteers around the world."

"Sounds rather like the Peace Corps. Do these student missionaries, as you call them, all teach?"

"No. Some work as nurses. Some teach in English Language schools, others in construction. Just about anything."

"Does your church send you by twos?"

"No. It just happened that this school needed two teachers. Each of us will have four grades with about fifteen students each."

After a time the woman leaned back in her seat and closed her eyes. Kara turned her attention to the frothy white clouds outside her window.

The faraway landscape reminded the girl of a

KARA

patchwork quilt that her mother had made. Just thinking about the quilt flooded her mind with memories. Unwillingly her thoughts drifted back through the years. First there had been the operation. Then the internal bleeding. Then came the rainy day when she, along with four older sisters and brothers, stood clustered about a newly dug grave in a secluded cemetery in the Bitterroot Mountains. Tears filled her eyes as she thought of the parent she had hardly known.

Four years old and motherless. Once again grief washed through her.

The girl's thoughts grew darker as she continued to remember. Some months after the funeral her father remarried. The oldest sister, reassured that her younger siblings would now be well taken care of, went ahead with her own plans for marriage and moved to another state. But for the next eight years Kara, along with one of her sisters, lived through one emotional storm after another.

Kara's eyes narrowed and she felt herself withdrawing, growing tense. Nervous. Scared. She shuddered as she recalled all too clearly the frequent violent drunken brawls between her father and stepmother. Each fight left the house in shambles, broken glass and potted plants strewn everywhere. Blood often ran down a chin from split lips, bruises appeared dark and swollen. Kara hid in dark closets, vainly trying to shut out the yelling and swearing by clasping her hands tightly over her ears. Even now she shivered involuntarily.

Taunted and teased by schoolmates she felt the sting of rejection as she listened to their singsong

HERE GOES

chants, "Drunkard's daughter, drunkard's daughter, nuthin' but a drunkard's daughter." She clenched her fists as if that would erase the memory of thoughtless children. Suddenly a new idea shot through her mind as she envisioned a headline in her hometown paper: "Drunkard's Daughter Turns Missionary." A smile played about the corners of her mouth. "That would make that Carla and her imps stand up and take notice!"

Eventually she went to live with Kathryn, her oldest sister. There she came to know the love of Jesus. She discovered what a home filled with His love could be like. No more fighting. No more cursing. No more violence. Hunger pains fled away. Only the nightmares remained to remind her of her violent childhood.

The plane banked, revealing a magnificent view of the Rockies. Jagged peaks, staggering beneath mounds of leftover snow thrust heavenward along the western horizon.

Kara's thoughts drifted back to the time when she first felt the desire to become a missionary. She'd been 12 then, learning to adjust to her new way of life. Shortly after her arrival a new minister came to the district, an aged veteran missionary from South America. Not only did he baptize Kara but he instilled within her a strong desire to return in his place to South America as a missionary.

She remembered listening with rapture to his tales of half-naked natives waving machetes menacingly, miraculous stories of angel-soldiers standing guard around the stranded missionary and his wife. Unconsciously Kara recoiled as she recalled his hair-raising description of the thirty-five foot anaconda lying like

KARA

a fallen log across the rugged jungle road.
During the next few years thoughts of South America were never far from her mind. Kara spent two years studying Spanish and avidly read every mission book on South America that she could find. But it was to a far different region that the Lord summoned the young girl.
She smiled wryly to herself. Her opportunity for mission service came from Majuro, a tiny coral atoll in the Pacific. The island would little resemble the steaming hot Brazilian jungles she had long dreamed about. It would have no lurking anacondas, voracious piranha, wild river rides, or encounters with stoic natives complete with bones through their ears and noses. Instead there would be . . . there would be . . . Her thoughts came to a screeching halt. "What would there be?"
Sharks? Cannibals? Students hungry for knowledge? Baptisms by the dozen? Whatever lay ahead, she determined that with the Lord by her side she could face anything. With sudden eagerness she began to look forward to her trek across the globe into the unknown.
Lynn joined her in San Francisco and together they flew to Hawaii where they changed planes for the last time. After a stop on tiny Johnston Island, Air Micronesia flew on to Majuro.
Gazing out the window, Lynn's thoughts flew back to her family in Kansas. She chattered blithely about home, family, big brothers, pets, and the farm she'd grown up on. Kara listened with amusement to her friend's animated voice. She felt drawn to Lynn's bubbly personality. Taller of the two and fairer-

HERE GOES

skinned, Kara had wavy chestnut hair and green eyes that contrasted with Lynn's dark eyes and black shoulder-length hair.

The girls craned their necks to peer out the tiny cabin window as they felt the plane descending. The loudspeaker crackled, followed by the charming accent of the Polynesian stewardess. "Please prepare for landing. Fasten your seatbelts. In just ten minutes we will be landing on the beautiful coral isle of Majuro, one of the thirty-two Marshall Islands. Fasten . . ."

The aircraft dropped lower and lower as it circled over the horseshoe-shaped island. Kara's eyes widened as she viewed how narrow it looked. Lynn voiced the panic she felt. "Where'll we land? All I can see is water. That island is no wider than a gravel road back home!"

"I surely hope there's a spot wide enough, otherwise we're in for a big swim!"

"That's not funny!" Lynn made some gurgling noises as the plane glided over the frothy whitecaps splashing across the surface of the bluish-green sea. "We're landing on the water!" she gasped as she gripped the armrests until her knuckles turned white.

The jet bounced several times before its wheels finally settled on the runway. Instantly the pilot braked and reversed thrust. The craft screeched to a halt next to a small steel-framed building. Kara stared out at the sea of brown faces peering expectantly up at the jet.

"Well, Lord," she whispered bravely, "here goes!"

Lizard Soup, Anyone?

2

A human-like scream pierced the night. Several more followed, each more hideous than the first. Kara's heart did flip-flops. Murder on the island? "I knew I should have stayed home, Lord! Why did I ever want to go as a missionary to this . . . this . . . lost island! Oooohhh! I wish I were back home. I don't want to be murdered!" Several paralyzing moments passed before the frightened girl recognized the unmistakable howls of tomcats fighting and screaming.

Plop! Something fell on the sheet. She tensed as she felt it wriggle its way up her arm. As she brushed the intruder away with her hands she shuddered. Whipping into a sitting position she squinted into the darkness to see a shadowy figure race across the sheet and disappear behind the bed. Glancing around the room by starlight Kara discovered many such ghostlike creatures scampering playfully about. One paused nearby and chirped. A friend answered from across the room.

Suddenly the girl smiled. "I know what you are. You're the geckos I was told about." Shaking a finger in warning at the pale creatures, she chided, "Don't you scare me like that again!" Lying down, she pulled the sheet over her head and drifted to sleep.

LIZARD SOUP, ANYONE?

"EEEEE-eeeeekkkkkk!"

Lunging from her bed, Kara toppled onto the floor as she tried to disentangle herself from the clinging, damp sheets. She saw Lynn jumping up and down on her bed, frantically waving her arms.

"Kara! Kara! Wake up! There's a spider! A *big* spider in my bed."

"Where?" Kara grabbed some paper. Rolling it up, she advanced warily toward her roommate's bed.

"There!" Lynn shrieked. "There he is!"

During the next several minutes Kara frantically chased the illusive spider as he played hide and seek in the rumpled sheets. At last she smacked him, much to Lynn's relief. But the girl screamed again. "What . . . what's that?" she gasped.

Kara smiled wanly. "Just a gecko. They're harmless."

"Looks like a lizard to me," the other student missionary wailed as she continued her spider dance atop her bed.

After shaking the sheets, the girls crawled gingerly back under the covers. Mosquitoes whined ominously in the darkness. Geckos chirped. From the jungle came other weird sounds.

"Kara?"

"Hmmm?"

"What do you think of the missionaries?"

"Well, I don't think Jan is happy about being here."

"Yeah, I get the impression that she never wanted to be a missionary in the first place. Can you believe that she actually called this island a desolate place? I think it's beautiful! The plumeria trees are simply gorgeous. And the smell of the blossoms on that tree is heavenly. Then there's the magnificent ocean."

KARA

Kara smiled in the darkness. "It is quite different from the prairie that we're used to seeing."

"And in one week school starts. What *do* we do to get ready? I don't know where to begin. My major is secretarial science and I don't know the first thing about teaching."

"I guess you could start by giving them typing lessons and after that you could begin shorthand . . ."

Lynn burst into giggles and Kara couldn't help but join her.

As Kara walked to the school building the first morning her step was light and eager. Along the path floppy red hibiscus flowers turned toward the dazzling sunlight. Giant breadfruit leaves shimmered around her. Graceful palm fronds danced the hula to welcome the new day. Snowy white fairy terns soared above the palm trees while coconut crabs skittered across the jungle path. All nature sang the joy she felt as she looked forward to her very first classroom of students.

Lynn, however, did not share her confidence. Nervously she sorted and resorted the papers on her desk. Picking up her lesson plan book she squelched the scream that rose in her throat and shuddered as a two-inch beetle scurried to a new hiding place. Bravely she picked up a fat dictionary and dropped it on the papers hiding the bug. But as the seemingly indestructible beetle wobbled away, limping, Lynn threw her hands up in despair. Glancing at her watch she snatched the school bell and rang it vigorously in the doorway.

Hearing the bell, Kara hurried to open her door but paused and offered a short prayer. "Well, Lord, here we are at last. You've finally made my lifelong dream come

LIZARD SOUP, ANYONE?

true. I'm a real missionary teacher. Please help me to have patience, kindness, and love in my heart for even the most unlovely student. Help me to make a difference in the lives of these children and most of all, Lord, please help me to draw them closer to You."

Swinging the door open wide, she beamed at the first student. But the room was empty. Only after she backed away from the door did the shy students start trickling silently in, slumping into the closest seats, avoiding the front row.

Just as Kara started to speak, in shuffled a tall, lanky boy, clad in faded blue jeans. A long, raveled shirttail hung past his hips. A ragged white headband held back the thick, black, shoulder-length hair from spilling into his pimply brown face.

"Mornin' teacher. My name is Colonel. What is your name?" he asked jauntily as he sauntered to an empty seat in front of her. In his hand he held a half-eaten lime. Kara felt her mouth puckering at the sight. A curious odor drifted to her nose. The boy's toenails were long, jagged, and dirty.

"You should not be late to school," she said, trying to appear professional and in control.

Cocking his head, Colonel grinned at his somber classmates and then up at his teacher. "I not be late," he piped. "These student here all be early."

Shyly the rest snickered.

Trying to keep a smile from creeping to the surface, she replied, "Try to be on time in the future."

Glancing across the roomful of thirty-six students, Kara felt a warm feeling of pride sweep through her. "My first classroom," she thought. About halfway through her welcoming talk Colonel waved his hand in

KARA

the air. Not waiting for her to respond, he stood and turned so he could speak both to her and to the class. "You talk very much too fast for these boy and girls. I will thanking you very much for you talk like these." Waving his arm like a music director's baton, he spoke extremely slow, nodding his head as he pronounced each word. "My name is Karanae. I am coming from the United State of Americas. I am happy to being your teacher. That is all. Time go home now." Grinning, the boy headed for the door.

Laughing, she grabbed him by the shoulder and piloted the boy back to his seat. Imitating him, she said, "You will sitting in your desk all these day."

And Colonel grinned.

As the last student filed out at the end of the day, Kara sighed happily. "If this is teaching—I'll love it!" Walking down the sidewalk to Lynn's room she popped in for a visit. Her smile faded as she noticed the stricken look on her roommate's face.

"It was awful!" the other girl wailed. "I've run myself ragged dashing from student to student. 'Leen, I need one help! Leen, I need one help!' They pronounce my name 'Leen.' And noise! They simply won't be quiet! I know I told them to be quiet ten thousand times today."

"I'm sure it will get better," Kara soothed as she bent to pick up some lime peelings.

"And the first graders. They can't speak any English! How am I supposed to teach them when we can't understand each other?"

"Maybe I could send some of the older girls down to help out now and then."

Lynn seemed to relax a bit. "I'm starved. Let's go up

LIZARD SOUP, ANYONE?

to the mission house and see if supper's ready."
　As the girls entered the back door the pastor's wife, Jan, inquired, "Well, girls, how was your day?"
　"Don't ask," Lynn moaned.
　"Oh Kara, you've already got a letter. Your mom must have sent it before you left."
　"Couldn't be from my mother," the girl replied softly. "She's dead." As she picked up the letter a smile rippled across her face. "It's from Paul!"
　Pastor Allen entered the room. "Must be a boyfriend from that look on your face."
　Lynn giggled. "Don't get her started on Paul. She'll never quit."
　Jan looked up from where she was setting the table. "Well, you know the old saying, 'Absence makes the heart to wander.' You might get back to the states and discover that he found himself another girlfriend."
　Kara scowled. "Not my Paul."
　"You might find I'm right." With that Jan set a pitcher of powered milk on the table. "Let's eat." Dressed in a sleeveless smock, she had drawn her brown hair into a tight bun. Housewife and mother of two preschoolers, the girls guessed that she greatly felt the absence of the modern conveniences that she'd left behind—the full-time electricity, hot water from the faucet, television, magazines, air conditioning . . . The way she spoke with such assurance about Paul upset Kara and a tiny fear of losing him began to nibble at the edges of her heart.
　The missionaries' two children, Sammy and Betsy, sat across the table from the two student missionaries. Shy little Betsy, with her big brown eyes, scarcely

21

spoke. But not Sammy. He hardly slowed down to catch his breath.

"Sure smells good," Lynn commented as she helped herself to the rice and egg gravy that Kara handed her. Lima beans, canned fruit, and bread completed the menu.

"When did your mother die?" Jan asked as she helped Betsy.

Kara felt all eyes turn to her as she answered quietly, "When I was four." Such questions made her uncomfortable for it always led to the inevitable.

"Who took care of you then?"

"My father remarried soon after."

"You mean you had a stepmother? Was she mean like Cinderella's?" Sammy demanded as he chewed a mouthful of rice.

"Sam, mind your manners," Pastor Allen told him.

Kara squirmed uneasily as she played with her peaches. "When I was 12 I went to live with my oldest sister and her family."

"Oh?" Jan raised her eyebrows. "How come?"

"Because my dad and stepmother were drunkards." There. It was out. Inwardly Kara begged that no one would ask any more questions.

Seeming to sense this, Lynn changed the subject by inquiring about the pastor's day.

Interrupting his adventures, Jan asked for the dish of lima beans. Taking a scoop she brought up a heaping serving spoon of beans and . . . To the amazement of all, a very limp gecko dangled from the spoon. With one accord, everyone's gaze shifted to their plates where the limas had once been.

"I think I'm going to be sick," Lynn whispered

LIZARD SOUP, ANYONE?

weakly as she made an abrupt exit.

Jan gagged.

Pastor Allen looked at the cooked gecko and then up at the ceiling and walls.

Kara gulped and finished her rice.

That evening she read Paul's letter by the light of a flickering lantern as the mission generator ran only a couple hours during the day. Eerie shadows danced across the gray cement walls. Suddenly Lynn's piercing scream shattered the air.

"What is it this time?" Kara gasped.

Scrambling frantically to the top of the small study desk, her roommate shouted, "A monster! There's a monster under my bed. I stepped on him!"

On Strike

---- 3 ----

Kara stared at the floor by Lynn's bed. "Are you sure you didn't step on your thongs? Or a gecko?"

Her roommate shuddered. "It was big and soft and wiggly. Like a snake."

"Can't be. There aren't any on the island."

The back door to the mission house slammed. Pastor Allen rushed down the pathway and banged on the girls' door. Throwing her robe on, Kara quickly unlatched the door and let him in. Lynn made little sense as she babbled on, so Kara quickly explained what had happened. The man shined his flashlight under both beds. Finding nothing he returned to the house.

After he left she patted Lynn's arm reassuringly, "Don't be afraid. Whatever it is, it won't hurt you. There's no poisonous animals on these islands."

But the other girl wasn't convinced. Long after Kara had fallen asleep she still lay stiffly on her bed, the sheet drawn up tightly under her chin.

Early the next morning the two teachers dressed by the light of a kerosene lantern. In the distance a dog howled an eerie, mournful tune. A ripened coconut fell with a loud bang on the tin roof and clattered noisily to the ground. The girls' room was the opposite end of the

ON STRIKE

shed that housed the electric generator. Unpainted cement block walls, two narrow wooden beds with thin mattresses, one small desk, and a small open closet completed their tiny quarters.

For days the two girls had been finding that they had to stay up extremely late and rise long before the sun in order to get their schoolwork and lesson plans finished. With four grades each and 36 students in a room they found themselves busier than they'd ever been before. To make less work Kara had combined some of the grades into one class, but still the tasks seemed unending. Lynn decided to suggest to Pastor Allen that he find another student missionary to come help. To their delight he agreed to request an additional one.

Once at the school Kara unlocked the door and stepped into her room. Shadows played about the walls as the light in the lantern flickered. Shadowy cockroaches and large beetles skittered nervously around, seeking shelter. Pigs from the nearby village rooted outside the window.

As Kara completed her paper work she kept one eye on the windows where she could watch the tropical world come awake. Palm trees, at first stark silhouettes against the reddish sunrise, turned lighter and lighter shades of green until they burst forth in splendor. Sunbeams danced across the leaves. After a quick breakfast at the mission house the girls hurried back to school to begin another day.

Just as Kara finished Bible class someone shuffled down the sidewalk toward her room. The visitor paused outside the windows and his black eyes peered in between the louvered windows. The boy's long,

KARA

thick, curly black hair bushed out behind his head, giving him a wild appearance. It was, of course, Colonel.

Kara swung the door open.

"How are you today, Karanae?" the boy asked cheerfully, not seeming to notice he was late as usual.

"Just fine, and you?"

"Just fine, just fine!" Sauntering into the room the boy slouched into his chair. In his hand he held a half-eaten lime.

"Colonel, did you bring a pencil to school today?"

"No," he admitted slowly as he sucked his lime. Taking out a rumpled napkin he opened it and sprinkled more salt on the morsel.

"What? You come to school with *no* pencil, *again*?" She clicked her tongue in despair. Every day since classes had started Kara had reminded him to bring one so he wouldn't have to borrow. Repeatedly he'd forgotten.

Colonel cocked his head. "Karanae, you bring one lime to school?"

"No."

Leaning forward he shook his finger at her. "What?" he exclaimed in mock surprise. "You come to school with *no* lime?" He clicked his tongue loudly.

The students tittered, and Kara couldn't help but laugh.

Glancing at her lesson plan book, she began giving assignments. As she was about to tell the seventh graders which math page to do, one of the fifth graders blurted, "These problem very much hard!"

One of the girls reached over and popped the boy in the shoulder. "They not hard. You just one lazy boy."

ON STRIKE

Smiling, Tayla, her long black hair cascading in waves below her slender shoulders, strolled gracefully to the front. "What page you want eight grade to do?"

As everyone started talking at once, Kara began to feel like a deflating balloon. What had happened to her nice, orderly, quiet students? Her eyes widened as she saw Marianne wad her paper and throw it impatiently on the floor. Her book followed with a flick of the wrist.

Kara clapped her hands for order and spoke sternly. For a time the students remained reasonably quiet. Then during the middle of the afternoon she noticed a haze in the room. Smoke swirled out from under her desk in the back of the room.

Snatching the burning garbage can away from her desk, Kara recoiled from the tongues of fire leaping out at her. Grabbing the small fire extinguisher hanging nearby, she forced herself to remain calm enough to read the operating instructions.

"Look! These fire he is all done!" Kendall exclaimed.

Turning, Kara saw curls of smoke drifting lazily toward the windows. Checking the can she saw that someone had dropped a social studies book directly on the flames, smothering them.

Fuzzy-haired Kendall grinned crookedly and muttered, "Silly teacher. Afraid of one small little fire." He clacked his tongue loudly as he sauntered to his desk.

Kara wondered what to do. How could she punish the culprit when she didn't know who it was? Deciding to tell the students to put their heads down on their desks, she lectured them soundly on proper school behavior.

During the next several days Kara felt as if her nice orderly classroom had gone through some sort of metamorphosis. Once meek and well-behaved, the students emerged from their cocoons as uncontrollable butterflies. Students, having asked to go to the small house (restroom), vanished into the jungle, to reappear at will or not at all. The noise level in the room rose daily.

Hordes of pesky mosquitoes swarmed around the sweating bodies in the hot classroom. Burning mosquito coils failed to make much of a difference. As Kara began a social studies lesson one afternoon she swatted one insect after another. At last she gave up and tried to ignore them. "Our island, Majuro, is one of the thirty-two Marshall Islands. The Marshalls are just south of the equator in the Pacific Ocean.

"Majuro is really the top of an underwater mountain. Tiny little coral animals called coral polyps, formed our island by building millions and millions of their homes on this mountain. After so long the coral poked above the water . . ."

Kendall rolled his eyes. "I not believing you. You say big lie! Majuro is island. Not mountain," he growled. "God made earth. Not coral plops."

"You one foolish teacher!" Colonel chided as he clicked his tongue in disgust.

"Have you ever seen that mountain we on?" Miles asked mischievously.

"No," Kara replied with a smile, "But special scientists, called oceanographers, have equipment to find this out. They send sound waves down to the ocean floor to measure how deep it is. That's how they can tell we're on a mountain."

"You bad woman!" Colonel wagged his finger in her

ON STRIKE

face. "You break one big commandment that say not to tell lie."

Rila, dark eyes smoldering, jumped from her chair. She reached over and yanked Colonel's hair. "You not call teacher bad woman."

"Well, if our island is not formed on top of a mountain, what holds it in place so it doesn't float around?"

"God hold it in His hand," Kendall blurted. "So it cannot float."

Kara stood speechless for several moments. "Yes, Kendall, you are so right, so very right. I can't argue with that." The simple trusting faith the boy exhibited had awed her. Later that day it amused her to overhear him repeating her social studies lecture to one of the smaller boys at recess time. When the boy expressed disbelief, Kendall shook the younger child roughly as he barked, "Kara tell truth. She one very wise teacher."

As she stood under a giant breadfruit tree she watched the students play volleyball. Gazing across the mission compound she soaked in the beauty of the island. Plush green grass carpeted the compound, creating the appearance that nature's carpet was soft when, in fact, broken shells and small bits of jagged coral made the ground uncomfortable to feet unaccustomed to walking barefoot.

Scattered breadfruit, papaya, and palm trees dotted the spacious compound surrounded by more palm trees towering above a dense jungle.

To Kara's right stood the yellow structure that housed the missionaries. Behind it was the shed containing the generator plant and the girls' room. Nestled by the mission house stood a water tank that

KARA

collected the rainwater that drained off the corrugated tin roof of the house. Clumps of hibiscus bushes graced the front.

To the far side of the compound, snuggled against the jungle, sprawled the three-room yellow cement block school. A second water tank stored the runoff from the school's roof.

One morning several days later Miles gazed longingly out of the windows, impatiently waiting for recess. Tall, dark, with wavy hair that always seemed to be in place, he was well-behaved and extremely intelligent. Often his black eyes twinkled with merriment while his face broke into a grin. At age 16 only one other boy stood taller and broader than he: Thompson.

A youth with dark, brooding eyes, Thompson remained aloof from Kara's attempts of friendliness. Seldom, if ever, did he smile.

When lunch began Miles begged her to give him the school's volleyball, promising that he would take good care of it. She agreed, thinking it would be nice not to have to gulp through her lunch so she could hurry back to school to give the boys the ball so they could play a game before classes resumed.

But just as the game started it ended abruptly. Pastor Allen appeared and snatched the ball. He ordered the boys to go home until it was time for school to begin again.

Disappointed and angry, they started to slink slowly away. Miles paused by the corner of the school and frowned. Nelson mumbled, "What wrong with that man? Kara gave the ball to us. He is not our teacher."

The group walked behind the schoolhouse and

ON STRIKE

slouched down on the sidewalk. Each face looked gloomier than the next.

"I no like these school. They no let us play," Thompson grumbled with a sour look, his dark eyes flashing in anger.

"Well, if we cannot play ball, we should not go to these school," Miles stated as he swatted a mosquito.

Nelson nodded in agreement. Short and stocky, the curlyheaded boy was Miles' best friend.

Slowly a grin began to spread across Colonel's brown face. "Let's go on strike!"

"Eman!" (good) the rest chorused as they all leaned back against the building. Folding their arms across their chests they sat in stony silence, determined not to move.

The Stranger

4

When Kara left the mission house she frowned to herself. Allen and Jan's ultimatum made her feel angry. She couldn't understand why they would not allow the students on campus at any other time than school or church hours. After all, she reasoned, wasn't the mission supposed to be what its name implied, a "mission" reaching out to all people all the time? Was a mission supposed to have working hours?

"I would far rather have the kids hanging around the mission than hanging around pool houses or at the theater soaking in Kung Fu movies," she had told them. But her meager attempts at reasoning were futile in the face of Jan's clinching statement, "That's the way it is." So Kara kept her angry thoughts to herself.

Lynn rang the bell just as she reached her classroom. Entering she found that the girls were present, but not a single boy.

"The boys they on strike," Tayla announced as she twisted her long hair into a braid that reached past her waist.

"They will not coming to these school no more," Marianne added.

"Why?"

THE STRANGER

"Maybe they not like these school," Tayla answered evasively.

"They are mad because Pastor Allen he took the ball from Miles. See? They are sit there." Marianne pointed out the back windows. With a mischievous grin the girl added, "Let them sit. We not need them boys."

The other girls giggled. Now Kara was angry. She bit the inside of her lip and wondered what she should do. If only Pastor Allen had left the boys alone to play a harmless game of volleyball. Sighing, she went around to the back of the school.

When they saw her coming they turned angrily away. Kara cringed as she heard the mumbled oaths and felt their icy glares. She'd seen the clenched fist Thompson had shaken at her as he turned his back on her.

"Go away from these place. We not listening to thing you say," Kendall growled.

Rising to his full height, Thompson took a step toward her, his face masked in anger. He raised his arm as if to strike her. Kara stared back into his smoldering black eyes even though he was taller and stronger. Suddenly he dropped his arm and slunk away into the jungle.

For a few stunned moments she remained frozen. It was as if she had stepped back in time and was once again a little girl, waiting for the blows to fall. She shivered.

Raising her eyes to those of Miles' she noticed that the anger had fled from his face. "Miles, I just found out what happened. It's all my fault and I'm sorry. I thought it would be all right to let you guys play a game. I'm really sorry. Please come back into the room." With a faint smile she added, "You won't gain a thing by staying back here except for a few mosquito bites."

Without a word Miles stood and headed for the classroom. The others followed. For now the crisis was over, but for how long? Kara stared into the jungle that had swallowed Thompson. Many times he had displayed a quick temper, but never before had he threatened to strike her.

Uncannily she realized she was not alone. Pinpricks of fear raced up her spine. Had Thompson returned? Whipping around she faced Miles. With a sigh she leaned back against the wall of the school, her heart beating wildly.

As if the tall boy read her mind he stated simply, "Don't worry. He will not hurt you. I make sure of that."

She looked deep into his dark eyes. With her whole heart she wanted to put her trust in him, but though the island was quite small, she knew that he could not be everywhere. Trying to cover her fear with a smile, she returned to the room with the boy.

As Kara entered Colonel blurted, "You one very bad teacher. I tell you many time you can no be late. Because you are coming late you can no be our teacher!"

Kendall seized an opportunity. Picking up the heavy, thick dictionary, he lugged it to the front of the room. "Now student, I will teach you many thing from these big book."

The laugh that Kara managed to smother helped to ease the tension.

Rila interrupted Kendall. "I no listen to you. You bad teacher."

THE STRANGER

"Jab keruru!" (hush up) the fuzzy-haired boy ordered. "Now, you must learn all word in these book from a to z."

"You are bwe bwe!" (crazy) Marianne grumbled. "There are too much word in these dictionary."

"Then you will make flunk these class!" Bowing low, he added haughtily, "I will not be your teacher no more. You are very naughty student."

As Kara presented the social studies lesson she noticed that Colonel did not copy the notes from the board. Telling him to do so, she turned back to the board as he wailed, "But I have no pencil."

She rummaged for one. "If you would only bring a pencil . . ."

He shrugged. "The little pencil, he no like to stay in my pocket."

Flipping a pencil through the air toward Colonel, Nelson offered eagerly, "Here. Use mine. I am tired to write these notes."

"Nelson!" his teacher gasped.

By the middle of the day Kara felt quite irritable. Kendall had changed the time on the clock which caused her to let out for recess far too early, then later Rila had pushed Colonel off his chair for making faces at her. During class Kendall and some other boys flew paper airplanes back and forth until she caught them. But one last plane managed to streak across the room, making a crash landing on her forehead. Kendall quickly fell to his knees to beg forgiveness. But at last she had had enough and ordered everyone to stay after school. Everyone groaned.

The minutes passed by, the ominous buzzing of mosquitoes the only sound to be heard. Suddenly

KARA

Colonel jumped to his feet and strode to the front of the room. With a flourish he declared, "Oh, Karanae, I am so sorry. I no want to hurt your feeling. You will not tell your boyfriend what naughty student are here?" Not waiting for an answer, he turned to the class and lashed forth, "You naughty student! Karanae come across the ocean to these school to teach us many thing. And then you act these way. I will tell your fathers and you will be spank very hard! No good you act these way. No good!" Switching into his native tongue he continued, shaking his long finger at the students. Then with a bow he sat down.

Silence.

Tears filled Kara's eyes as the last student left the room. "They are not bad students," she tried to reassure herself. "Just so full of mischief."

At supper she was totally unprepared for Jan's sharp tongue.

"Kara, from now on, those kids are not allowed on the compound except during school and church hours. You may not agree, but that's the way it is." She continued for several minutes. Waving a mixing spoon for emphasis, she added, "And another thing. Your room is far too noisy. And it's like Grand Central Station the way your students parade in and out of your room all day."

"But they have to go to the bathroo . . ."

"Let one go at a time. You need to take a lesson from Lynn. Her room is much quieter than yours. She's consistent with her discipline. She *makes* them mind. She doesn't tolerate foolishness."

Her mind in a whirl, Kara replied, "How do you think I should enforce discipline differently?"

THE STRANGER

"Lynn uses a stick on hers. If I were you I'd use a belt. That would shape those big boys up."

Kara bristled. Employ a belt on students 15 and 16 and almost as big as her five feet seven inches? Unthinkable. And to be compared to Lynn who wasn't even an elementary education major? Holding her anger in, she ate her lunch in silence and excused herself before the others finished.

She fled down a secluded jungle path where she found refuge under a plumeria tree. Her thoughts raced wildly. What Jan said held some truth, but what could she do? Quiet sobs shook her slender shoulders. "What do I do?" she moaned over and over. "I . . . I can't whip them. That would be awful. If I did I'm afraid I'd . . . I'd . . . end up like Daddy!" she blurted out to a gecko that peeked curiously at her from under a leaf. "When he'd get drunk his fists flew. He'd hurl plants. Dishes. Chairs. Even the telephone. I can't get angry! I'd fly into a rage. Then my students would be afraid of me like I am of my Dad. Oh, what do I do, Lord?" Deciding the conversation wasn't meant for him, the gecko slipped into the foliage.

The next day Colonel, Thompson, and Kendall were absent. No doubt playing hooky, she grimly thought to herself. The day passed quietly. When school ended she hurried to join Lynn and the missionaries for a quick trip into town at the other end of the island.

For over a half hour Kara let the wind whip through her hair, blowing her troubles away as she perched on the wheel hump in the back end of the pickup.

One lone paved highway ran the full length of the narrow horseshoe-shaped island. With less than five square miles, the island stretched like a piece of yarn

KARA

winding across a blue quilt for 30 miles. Sections of the island were so narrow that at times both the ocean and lagoon washed up on the road.

Palm trees, scaveola bushes, and other jungle flora lined the highway, separating it from the billowing ocean waves that often sent sprays of water splashing across the road. In a year's time the daily rains added up to about 120 inches, making the island a lush tropical paradise. But even so its inhabitants had to conserve water for the drier months when the rains failed to come.

The temperature and humidity hovered in the eighties. Such hot, damp heat made the missionaries feel like cooked noodles.

The island had a population of about 8,000 people, most of whom lived at either end where it widened. The Adventist mission was located at one end next to a boarding high school operated by the Assemblies of God church. At the opposite end of the island was the larger Catholic mission. There the islanders flocked to do their shopping. There the streets teemed with taxis, people, and barking dogs. Stores crowded the roads. Flies swarmed about garbage cans and open doorways. Radios blared. Taxis honked. Little children dashed carelessly across the pavement after runaway balls. Teenagers hung around the store steps. Old men smoked pipes as they squatted lazily on the sidewalks. Fat old women dressed in their brightly flowered muumuus meandered in and out of the stores or squatted on the porches, their billowy dresses pulled up modestly between their legs.

First stop was the post office. Excitement ran high as Allen returned with a handful of mail. Kara fairly

THE STRANGER

pounced on three letters from Paul. "Not five this week?" Allen teased. "Only three? Too bad."

For a few minutes everybody read their mail. Then the pastor announced, "Looks like we're going to have somebody new around."

"Another student missionary?" Lynn asked hopefully.

"Nope. This young man will be working for the government schools. And he's single. Here's your chance girls."

Just then a strange voice startled the group. Turning, they faced a tall, blond, and very thin man. Bright blue eyes sparkled like sapphires on either side of a long nose. A cocky blue sailor's cap tried to hold straight blond hair back from his eyes. The stranger wore a sleeveless shirt and cut-offs revealing bony knees and hairy legs.

He held out his hand and grinned. "Hi, my name is Ronn Jacobson. I couldn't help overhearing, so I knew I'd found the right group."

Pastor Allen apologized profusely. "I'm sorry we weren't able to meet you at the airport. We just now received this letter telling of your arrival." He proceeded to introduce the others.

Kara's eyes narrowed. Why had this tall stranger suddenly appeared in their midst? Where did he come from? Why was he really here? Crazy questions flitted through her mind. A feeling of shame swept through her for thinking such thoughts, but something about him made her feel extremely uneasy. She felt further dismayed when Jan invited him to the mission for the coming weekend.

Ronn accepted graciously. Tipping his hat, he

strode down the sidewalk, head and shoulders taller than the natives swarming around him.

Allen chuckled. "Are we ever in for an exciting weekend!"

"Now Kara," his wife said, "just because you already have a boyfriend doesn't mean you can't check this guy out. No doubt Paul has a string of girlfriends back at college. If I told you once I told you a dozen times, 'absence makes the heart to wander.' "

"Not Paul," she said quietly.

"Already he's writing less. That's a sure sign."

Kara squirmed miserably.

"Ronn seems to be very nice. Not bad looking. A bit thin. But friendly. And," she added with emphasis, "he's here."

Wanting to avoid further confrontation, Kara turned and went into the nearest store.

Jan glanced at the other student missionary. "Did I say something wrong?"

Lynn's dark eyes flashed. "At least a dozen things." Then she too, left.

Finding Kara, she put her arm around the distraught girl's waist. "Just ignore her," she whispered.

"Why does she have to be so. . . so. . ."

"Cold?" Lynn finished. "Maybe one of her boyfriends jilted her. Maybe she thinks she's really trying to help in her own way. . ." She giggled, "Besides, who's the one without a boyfriend, anyway?"

Kara smiled. "He's all yours!"

After church that weekend Kara went to her room to change her shoes. Lynn was already there, only too eager to talk about Ronn. As Kara bent to get her thongs under the bed she gasped.

THE STRANGER

"What's the matter?"

Not wanting to frighten Lynn further, she stammered, "A gecko must have startled me."

Now Kara felt frightened. Whatever it was under there was much bigger than a gecko. No wonder Lynn had screeched that night.

Mr. Know-It-All

5

Sabbath evening the mission family, Ronn, and the two student missionaries relaxed about the living room after a hectic day. Pastor Allen conducted two church services every Sabbath, one at each end of the island. Both met in schoolrooms or, on nice days, out under the trees because the Adventists as yet had no church buildings. The soaring temperatures and high humidity always sapped the missionaries' strength, making such busy Sabbaths a real challenge. Such times helped Kara realize why life in tropical places ran at a slower pace than what she was accustomed to back in the States.

After sharing tales of his many travels and adventures throughout the world, Ronn suggested that everybody go hunting for shells that evening. According to the tide schedules there would be an extremely low tide, exposing more beach and potential shells than usual.

With the exception of Jan and her little girl, the rest made a mad scramble to hunt for swimsuits, flashlights, and net bags. Jumping into the pickup, the excited group drove to the end of the island. The naked beach stretched far out, leaving a multitude of tidal pools, some quite wide and deep. In the distance one could hear the muffled sound of the ocean pounding

MR. KNOW-IT-ALL

on the reef and see the dim outline of the exposed reef, and the faint silhouette of an outer island. Aside from the bobbing flashlights of the beachcombers, the brilliant stars were the only source of light.

Sharing a flashlight, Kara and Lynn picked their way out toward the reef. Gasping delightedly, Lynn bent and seized a round piece of coral. "Oooohhh! How pretty!"

"That's mushroom coral. Soak it in purex for a few hours and it will look snowy white."

As Lynn put her coral into a net bag she squealed again.

Ronn splashed up to the girls. "What'd you find?"

Lynn stood up. "I don't know, but it's marvelous!"

"That's a spi . . ."

As if Ronn didn't hear Kara he excitedly interrupted, "It's a Lambis Chiragra conch, commonly called Spider conch."

She bit her tongue. Until Ronn's arrival she had been the only authority on shells. Jealousy welled up inside her, then instant guilt followed as she reminded herself that missionaries shouldn't have such feelings, but the feeling persisted. Kara turned and frowned into the darkness. Ronn acted as if he knew everything there was to know about shells. He even flaunted scientific names. "What a show off," she muttered.

"What's that?" Ronn asked as he turned to her.

"Oh, nothing."

Just then little Sammy came running. Suddenly he tripped and splashed everybody. Jumping up quickly, he showed them the large shell he had found.

"That's a Horned Helmet conch," Ronn stated. "These shells live in shallow tropical waters on sandy bottoms around the world. They feed on sea urchins."

"That would be like trying to eat a porcupine—quills and all!" Lynn giggled.

Some of these Helmets get up to ten inches."

Lynn turned to Kara. "Did you know that?"

"I knew they got quite large," the other girl answered stiffly.

Pastor Allen appeared with a shell in his hands. "Say, this looks like a Turk's turban."

"That's what it is, a turban shell," Kara stated.

When the pastor looked to Ronn for confirmation, Kara rolled her eyes in disgust.

"She's right. This shell . . ."

His words faded as Kara waded away. "I 'spose Mr. Know-it-All knows the scientific names for the stars, even," she sputtered as she paused by a knobby coral head. She thought of Paul. "I wonder if he is thinking about me?" Pangs of homesickness stabbed her as she envisioned the rolling prairie back home, the sun rising over a nearby butte, the smell of pancakes on the griddle . . . an unseen tear slipped down her cheek.

The next couple of hours went on much the same. Somebody would find a shell and go running to Ronn who whipped out scientific names, common names, and facts like he was a walking encyclopedia. Kara suddenly felt left out.

Once when she was explaining to Sammy how the mantle made the cowrie shells so shiny, Ronn approached. Kara ignored him and kept doggedly on her lecture to the little boy.

"Are these Tiger cowries, too?" Sammy asked as he brought forth several little shells.

"They're cowries, but not Tiger cowries."

MR. KNOW-IT-ALL

"They're called Money cowries," Ronn informed him. "Know how they got their name?"

"If *you* know, why don't *you* tell him," Kara stated icily.

While he explained she chided herself for her reaction. "Why do I let him upset me so?" she wondered. "Why can't I like him?"

Ronn tried to start a conversation with her. "You know quite a bit about shells, don't you?"

"I suppose so."

"How'd you manage that? You don't live anywhere near the ocean."

"You don't have to live beside the ocean to learn something about shells." Turning, she waded away.

Lynn arrived just in time to hear Kara's last remark. "Her grandmother lived near the coast and started her on a shell collection," she explained. "I guess she has several hundred shells."

"I get the distinct impression that she doesn't like me. Have I offended her?"

"No. I think she misses her boyfriend. Jan's always giving her a bad time about 'absence makes the heart wander.' "

"I see. If she's friendly to me, then Jan will think her heart is wandering from lover boy." He chuckled softly.

Glancing back, Kara saw the two still talking. As they laughed, she frowned to herself. She tried to sort through her mixed feelings about Ronn. Why couldn't she like him? How she wished she had someone to talk to. Lynn was out of the question since she liked the guy.

Glancing up at the sky, Kara felt suddenly very alone. Then into her mind flashed a verse, "I am with you alway . . . even to the ends of the earth." A warm feeling of God's love seemed to wrap itself around her as she realized she really was not alone. She did have Someone to go to. Bowing her head, she brought her problem involving Ronn to the Lord. Somehow and someway He would help her.

Several days later Kara walked aimlessly along the ocean at the end of a trying day at school. A barrier of scaevola bushes bordering the shoreline stopped the salty spray from blowing inland and killing the less hardy plants. The salty sea spray rolled off the waxy, stiff scaevola leaves like water beads off a newly waxed car.

The thundering of the ocean waves on the reef usually drowned any trouble pounding in her heart —but not today. The sea lay calm. Like an enormous mirror it stretched endlessly before her. Troubled, she pondered over and over the events of the day. Thompson's belligerence had finally exploded. In anger he had thrown the small classroom clock across the room, smashing it against the wall. Pastor Allen had recommended his dismissal from school, but Kara wondered if that were the only way to deal with troublemakers. Wasn't there a better one?

After spending time in prayer over the matter she wandered back to the mission. Then hearing the distant sound of shattering glass, she stopped abruptly on the path. Alarm swept through her as she realized the noise came from the direction of the school. Hurriedly she raced down the overgrown jungle path. Rounding the corner at the back of the school building, she froze. With shock and surprise she gazed at the scene before her.

MR. KNOW-IT-ALL

Gripping a knife in his strong hand, Thompson slashed at the windows, knocking the glass louvers from their slots. The glass smashed on the cement.
"Thompson!"
Abruptly the boy turned, knife held mid-air, as if wondering whether to run or not. But his face hardened and he stared unflinchingly at his teacher as if daring her to do something to stop him.
Kara's mind whirled. "Thompson," she croaked, "put that knife down!"
Icily he sneered at her as he stepped forward, waving the gleaming knife in her face.

Help!
I Can't Swim!

6

With a gasp, she started slowly backing up, her legs feeling like cooked noodles. Frantically she prayed.

"Thompson, um . . . a . . . you, um, put that knife a . . . away. Somebody could get hurt."

"Maybe you," he muttered. His dark eyes smoldered and his lips curled viciously.

Hearing footsteps behind her, Kara glanced over her shoulder. Relief flooded through her as she recognized Nelson and Miles running toward her. Nelson took up position next to her, his fists flexing. Beside him stood Miles, his shoulders squared back, arms at his side, a fierce look upon his face. Then stepping forward, he spoke briskly in Marshallese.

Thompson muttered something but Kara didn't understand what either had said. Quietly Nelson whispered, "Miles say he must fight him—not you."

"No!" she shouted without thinking. "No! You mustn't fight!"

Nelson put his arm out to stop her as she rushed forward. "No," he cautioned. "Thompson, he will not fight Miles. He much afraid to fight him. Miles is relative to king of island. He be in big trouble if he fight king family. No, Thompson will not fight him."

Suddenly Thompson lowered the arm that held the

HELP! I CAN'T SWIM!

knife and slunk into the jungle.

Feeling faint, Kara pressed a hand against the side of the building to steady herself. Nelson patted her shoulder. "We hear he come to make trouble so me and Miles we hurry."

"Thank you," she breathed. Would Thompson really have hurt her if the boys hadn't come?

Miles faced her. "Thompson is one very bad boy. Make too much trouble. He is always too much angry."

The frantic voice of Pastor Allen as he dashed around the corner now interrupted them. "What happened? I heard glass . . ." His mouth dropped wide open as he viewed the damage. Angrily he demanded, "Who did this?"

"Thompson," Nelson answered.

"That boy is a barrel of trouble. We don't need his kind in this school. He will be dismissed." Whirling about, he left.

"Why you not tell Allen about the knife?" Miles asked.

Kara shrugged. "He won't try to hurt you boys now, will he?"

"He will not fight us."

As Kara cleaned up the mess she did some serious thinking. With a sinking feeling she realized that she had lost control of discipline in her room—but how to get it back? Suddenly an idea popped into her head. Whipping out construction paper and other materials she worked through supper and the rest of the evening. At last she stood back and observed her handiwork.

A paper bird cage projected out from the bulletin board. Inside sat a jailbird dressed in black and white stripes. Around its neck hung a sign with one word, "Tomfooler." Below the bulletin board Kara had placed a single chair with a long bookshelf fencing it off from the rest of the room. A large sign labeled "Tomfooler" hung on the back of the chair.

"That should do the trick. Nobody will want to be isolated in that chair." As a little girl she remembered shunning her classroom's dunce chair. Perhaps it might work here.

Walking into the room the next morning Kendall paused by the chair. Scratching his head he asked, "Who is these Tomfooler boy? I not hear his name on these island."

After everyone had sat down Kara began her story. "Once there was a boy named Tom. He was very lazy and naughty . . ."

Nelson leaned forward and poked Colonel. "Maybe like you!"

Colonel grinned and yawned loudly.

". . . He would do anything to get out of a job. He only wanted to fool around. His aunt spanked him many times each day. Soon he became known as 'Tomfooler' because he always fooled around. Since none of us want to be bad like this Tom and called 'Tomfooler,' let's all do our work and behave. If you are caught fooling around or being bad, you will have to sit in this Tomfooler chair."

The students sat quietly for some time until Kara smugly felt her plan was already working.

A little later Miles picked up the Kleenex box. Parading up and down the aisle, he called, "Five cents a paper. Five cents a paper."

"Miles! Put that box down and go to your seat!"

HELP! I CAN'T SWIM!

Looking slyly at her out of the corner of his eyes, he asked mischievously, "Am I Tomfooler now?"

Her mouth dropped open. "You aren't supposed to want to be Tomfooler!"

Later that morning she caught Kendall drilling a hole in the cement with a carbide rod from science class. "It works! It really does drill through cement."

"Kendall!"

"Is he Tomfooler now?" Marianne inquired.

Without waiting for an answer Kendall hopped over the bookshelf and plopped into the Tomfooler chair. Instantly the students burst into gales of laughter and tauntingly called, "Tomfooler!" "Kendall is one Tomfooler now!" "He one lazy bad boy always making foolishness!"

Kendall merely grinned and leaned lazily back in his chair.

Kara threw up her arms in despair. "Oh, where did I go wrong!"

As the students left that day she couldn't help smiling. "The good times far outweigh the bad," she mused to herself.

The following weekend Ronn again stayed at the mission. "It's beginning to become a habit," Kara thought. But even so he helped liven up the group with his tales of adventure. Sunday morning the group decided to go to the beach after breakfast.

As Lynn emerged from her room she screamed and jumped to one side. Ronn scrambled to her rescue, followed closely by Jan and Allen. Kara raced around the corner of the house. All stared at the enormous black lizard sunning itself on the girls' doorstep.

"I've never seen such a big lizard!" Allen exclaimed.

KARA

"That must be our monster," Kara said thoughtfully, remembering the times the shadowy creature had frightened them at night.

"He's over a foot long," Ronn estimated.

Lynn shuddered as Ronn guided the reptile toward the jungle.

Afterwards Ronn chuckled as he listened to Lynn describe her previous encounters with the elusive lizard. Kara watched them through narrowed eyes.

Once at the beach Allen donned snorkeling equipment and headed out toward the reef. Jan spread a towel for sunbathing. Their children played in the shallow water. As Ronn slipped his flippers on he noticed the girls watching him. "Where's your snorkels and fins?"

"We don't have any," Lynn replied. "Neither of us can swim."

After much persuasion and tales of how beautiful the underwater sea world was, Ronn finally talked Kara into trying it with his extra set of snorkeling equipment. He repeatedly assured her that she didn't need to know how to swim. All she had to do was float and paddle her feet. It sounded easy enough.

When he had her outfitted he showed her how to move her arms, hold her mouth over the mouthpiece, and kick her feet. Timidly she waded into the warm salty waters of the lagoon. She felt a bit chagrined when Ronn remained friendly in the face of her hostility.

At last she reached deeper water. Swinging her arms in wide arcs, she paddled her flippers and glided forward. For a moment she almost turned back, but the desire to view the sea world was stronger. Up

HELP! I CAN'T SWIM!

ahead the sandy bottom changed into a thick forest of coral.

Colorful coral formations of many shapes and sizes crowded the ocean floor. Her presence frightened away a tiny octopus. Little blue fish darted in and out of a gently waving sea anemone. Shells of all descriptions dotted the sand and crevices in the coral. Kara longed to be able to dive down and retrieve them.

Suddenly she saw Ronn pointing at an exquisite fish. Shaped like a pancake on end, it was brilliantly yellow with a pointed snout. Overcome with excitement she opened her mouth to speak. Too late, she realized what she'd done. Instantly her mouth filled with salty sea water. Flailing her arms frantically, she sank under the water.

Ronn
to the Rescue

7

Kara clawed her way to the surface of the lagoon only to slip beneath the water again. "Oh, Lord!" she prayed, "Help me! I can't swim!"

She surfaced with a splash. Flailing her arms, she gasped for air only to plunge deeper and deeper, choking on salty seawater. Visions of her family, Paul, friends back at college, all flashed through her mind. Then vaguely she became aware of something jerking her upwards. Just as she felt herself passing out she burst above the water. Coughing and sputtering she gasped for air, her heart hammering wildly.

"You ok?" Ronn asked as he supported the shaking girl while he tread water.

Breathing heavily, Kara continued to cough and sputter as she pushed her wet hair away from her eyes. Dimly she realized Ronn must have pulled her goggles from her face. Trembling with fright she gasped, "Oh Ronn! I forgot and opened . . ."

"I should never have encouraged you to come out here, knowing you couldn't swim."

"You never forced me. I wanted to."

"Still, I shouldn't have been so persistent. You could have drowned!" His grasp on her waist tightened as he added, "You nearly scared me to death!"

She looked into his steel-blue eyes. Guilt clutched

her as she remembered the way she'd treated him since his arrival. And for what reason? Conscience smitten, she whispered, "Thank you. Thank you for saving my life! I'll never forget it. Never."

"Whoa now! All I did was what any nice guy would have done."

"You really are a nice guy. I'm sorry I've treated you so badly. I don't know what got into me. I'm a missionary. Missionaries aren't supposed to act that way."

"Apology accepted. But since when did missionaries become so perfect?"

Her eyes widened. How did he know her feelings of incompetence? Finding her voice she sputtered, "Because . . . because they just are!"

Ronn shook his head. "No wonder you have trouble coping. Trying to be perfect in an imperfect world." He smiled. "Ease up on yourself. Just do your best. That's all the Lord expects. Think you can make it back now?"

She nodded grimly. "If you stay close by."

Lynn shook her head in disbelief as she listened to their tale. It shocked her even more to observe Kara putting the flippers and goggles back on.

Ronn stuck his thumb up in the air. "Thatta' girl, Kara! Conquer your fear—don't let your fear conquer you." He could not but help noticing that she paused as she entered the water and that her hands trembled.

On the next trip to town both girls bought a set of snorkeling equipment.

Later that afternoon Kara took a spill on the sharp, jagged coral on the oceanside. An incoming wave knocked her down and rolled her over and over across its sharp surface. When she scrambled to her feet, blood streamed in rivulets down her arms and legs. Lifting a throbbing hand she gulped in dismay at a gaping gash on her palm.

She limped back to the mission, leaving Lynn on the lookout for Ronn who was diving out over the reef. Pastor Allen and Jan whipped out the first aid kit and started to work. Coral cuts, like knife wounds, bled freely, so she looked much worse than she really was. Sore and miserable Kara decided not to return to the ocean. Instead she headed toward the school.

For several hours she worked without interruption. Then the door opened and in popped Ronn's blond head. "Mind if I come in?"

"Not at all. I could use a break."

Taking a seat, he sprawled his long legs out in front of him.

"You're an English teacher, Ronn, how do you teach these kids adjectives and the use of commas in these language textbooks when they can't even speak proper English?"

"If I were you I'd throw these stateside English books away."

"Seriously?"

Ronn nodded. "You've got to teach these kids how to speak English before they can learn some of this other stuff."

"How?"

For the next hour while she carefully took notes he gave her pointers on how to go about doing it. As Ronn summed up some of the ideas, she laughed, "I think we've got it, Professor Jacobson!"

Abruptly he asked, "Why didn't you like me at first?"

Her face reddened. "I . . . I'm not really sure," she

RONN TO THE RESCUE

began hesitantly. "I felt kind of suspicious of your sudden appearance out here in the middle of nowhere. Then, too, I thought if I acted friendly to you that . . ."

"People would think your heart was wandering away from your boyfriend?"

Kara's blush deepened.

"I've heard Jan's caustic remarks. And I want you to know that being friends with me is not showing disloyalty to Paul. Just because you're a girl and I'm a guy doesn't mean that we can't be friends and leave it at that." He smiled.

She shook her head in wonder. "How is it you understand me so well? You've put into words exactly what I've been thinking. And you did the same thing back at the lagoon. You hit it right on the nose about my problem that missionaries had to be perfect. I felt so frustrated because I couldn't measure up to what I thought they had to be like. In the mission books, and I read every single one, the missionaries seemed perfect. They never felt jealous, discouraged, incapable . . . like me," she whispered softly. "And if they did, they flew to their knees and presto! Everything was all right."

"Guess I've just had more experience dealing with people than lots of folks have."

"It's nice to have someone to talk to," she admitted shyly.

"You usually bottle things up, don't you?"

She meekly nodded.

"That's not good. Volcanoes do that and eventually they erupt. Sometimes when we don't vent our feelings a lot of anger and frustration can build up."

"Anger is wrong."

KARA

"Anger is a feeling. It isn't right or wrong. The way people act out their anger can be wrong, though."

Kara frowned. She pulled at a lock of her shoulder-length brown hair. "But I . . . I . . . can't show anger. I can't scream and shout. To me that's wrong. I cringe inside when someone yells at me."

"Who said you had to yell and scream to show anger?"

She shrugged. Ronn remained silent for several minutes. At last he said, "I could be wrong, but was one of your parents an alcoholic?"

Stunned, she stared at him. Gathering her wits, she faintly replied, "Both my dad and stepmother are drunkards. How did you know?"

"I know lots of people whose parents were alcoholics, and you have some of their characteristics. You're afraid to trust people, you don't share your feelings, and I'd venture to say, you're afraid to love someone."

"But I do love someone—Paul!"

"As long as he doesn't get too close."

Suddenly Kara wished Ronn would go away. He talked too much about things she seldom even let herself think about. Doing so opened a dark closet filled with horrendous memories. Like now. It would make the nightmares begin all over again.

The screaming, bloody fights. Dark, foreboding basements filled with their own terror. Taunts of cruel children. Reckless, drunken rides along high mountain roads with sheer drop-offs.

As for Paul, she wondered if Ronn could possibly be right? She knew it was far easier to write, "I love you" in a letter than say it to Paul's face. And what about anger? *Could* there be a right way to display it? Out

RONN TO THE RESCUE

loud she asked, "OK, how do I do it?"

"Like with Jan?"

Kara nodded.

"Confront her. Tell her how you feel."

"I can't. She'd yell louder or throw something at me."

"Jan is not your father or your stepmother." He gave her time to let the words soak in. "Maybe you could approach her later when she's calmed down and you've had time to think. Begin with, 'I feel threatened when you yell because . . .' or 'I'm having a hard time coping with your anger. I could accept your advice better if you'd talk quietly and listen to what I had to say.'

"A person doesn't have to knock someone around or yell to show anger," he continued. "Anger does not have to lead to violence. It is simply a feeling, and by communicating it you can relieve a lot of tension. Remember, if you don't tell people when they upset you, how will they know if something is wrong?"

Kara wanted to believe him. She longed to be able to express herself the way he was describing. It sounded so simple. Yet too frightening to attempt. It would be hard to open up after holding everything in for so long. A Scriptural passage flashed into her mind: "My grace is sufficient for thee." But could it erase the hurts and anger of the past? Suddenly Kara realized with some shock that she even had trouble trusting the Lord. Ronn was right again. She was afraid to trust. Afraid to love.

Later, as he rose to leave, Kara told him, "Thanks for coming, Ronn."

"Friends?" he asked as he held out his hand.

Shaking his hand, she nodded emphatically, "Friends."

No sooner had she spoken then a blood curdling cry shattered the air. Ronn swung the door open. "That came from the mission house!"

"Jan?" Kara gasped. But he didn't answer for he was already halfway across the compound.

Typhoon!

8

As Kara rounded the corner of the mission house she met Jan staring straight ahead as if in shock. Kara followed her gaze, only to have nausea sweep through her. Dangling from a noose swung the missionaries' black mother cat, a stick speared through its body.

The woman finally found her voice. "Who would murder a poor, defenseless cat! If I ever found out who did this I'd . . . I'd . . ." She burst into tears. The children clung to her skirt, staring wide-eyed at their pet.

Her husband put his arms around her shoulders. "Barbaric!" she sobbed. "Oh, Allen! We've got to go back home! We can't raise our children in a place like this. It's uncivilized. There's no telephone. The hospital is deplorable. The doctors are glorified witch doctors. There's no electricity. Nothing! I want to go home!" Her shoulders shook uncontrollably. Without a word he ushered her into the house.

Ronn cut the noose, then buried the cat while the girls stood silently by.

For the first time Kara began to realize something of the turmoil which the missionary's wife must be going through. It couldn't be easy raising children in a strange place. No wonder Jan was short-tempered and easily frustrated.

KARA

Just prior to Christmas the pastor and his family left the island for a much needed vacation. The girls found themselves in charge of the mission in their absence. Everything ran smoothly for the first few days—then everything went wrong.

"What are we going to do!" Kara wailed. "First the generator breaks down and Allen isn't here to fix it so there's no lights, no radio, no record player, and now there's no fridge! I give up trying to light that stubborn little pilot light underneath it." Wiping the dripping sweat from her brow she rose to her feet.

Wisps of black hair, unwilling to stay entwined in a bun clung to Lynn's sweaty neck as she slumped in a chair nearby. "This heat is unbearable. And the humidity! Everything feels so clammy and damp. No wonder everything gets moldy." She fanned herself. "Maybe we should go to the Assemblies of God Mission down the road. Allen says that they have a good maintenance man. Perhaps he could fix the generator and this goofy refrigerator."

In no time at all Mike peered carefully at each piece of the generator. Finding some corroded wire he sadly shook his head as he informed the girls that an electrician would need to repair it. Going to the kitchen he expertly lit the pilot light on the kerosene fridge. As he was about to leave a vehicle came screeching to a halt in the gravel driveway. A wiry man popped his balding head in the door.

"Mike! We need you to help batten down the buildings at the high school. Warnings for a typhoon are out. It's expected to arrive anytime!"

Kara and Lynn exchanged glances of horror. A typhoon? One of those dreaded tropical hurricanes

TYPHOON!

that could rage for days, leaving in its wake death and destruction? Kara found her voice first. "How, um, d . . . do we get ready for a typhoon?"

"You girls alone?" Mike asked in surprise. When they nodded, he glanced about the room. "Since you don't have wooden shutters on your windows, I suggest you shut the windows on one side of the house. Keep in a sheltered part—away from any windows that could shatter in high winds. Other than that, there's not much you can do—except pray." As he left he added, "You should be quite safe in this house. It's one of the best built on the island."

As the men left, scattered raindrops started to fall. Large black clouds loomed ominously all over the western sky. The moon and stars hid as if to escape the forthcoming wrath of the elements. Geckos chirped nervously. Boobies and gannets sought refuge in their nests beneath the thick foliage of trees and bushes. The turbulent sea would send fishes scattering to protective rocky crags. Only the palm trees could not seek safety from the impending storm.

For a few stunned moments the girls stood immobile. Then they flew into action. Dashing to the windows Lynn cranked some shut while Kara opened others. Together they pulled furniture away from the windows. Picking up the stereo they set it back in a sheltered corner of the hallway and covered it with a sheet of plastic. Gathering blankets, kerosene lanterns, matches, and crackers, the girls dumped them in the hall beside the stereo.

"What else?" Lynn asked. "Oh, I wish Ronn were here. He'd know what to do."

Kara paced the room, then paused in front of the

window. Tree limbs danced in the windy darkness. Heavy rains pelted the glass, driving water in through tiny cracks around the frames. Moisture trickled like teardrops down the wall beneath the windows.

For a moment Kara wished that she was home back in the states—safe from the typhoon. But even as she thought it she knew that she was just where she wanted to be. Here. Close to her students. Would they be safe during the storm? In spite of their escapades she felt attached to each one just like they were family.

She envisioned the raging winds and heavy rains battering their flimsy shelters. Most of the island's people lived in little shacks built from scraps of wood and remnants of sheet metal from the war.

Suddenly she became aware of Lynn's presence. At first she couldn't understand what the other girl was saying, but the words finally took shape and softly Kara joined her in repeating, ". . . He who dwells in the shelter of the Most High will rest in the shadow of the Almighty . . . " The words took on new meaning as they lived through their own "terror of the night." The Psalm turned into a prayer as the girls claimed the words, "He will call upon me, and I will answer him, I will be with him in trouble, I will deliver him."

A coconut thudded on the roof, snapping the girls into action. Both made a hasty exit to the sheltered hallway where they huddled on the floor, pulling the blankets about them, shivering not so much from the cooler winds as from fear.

Whistling and howling, the wind tore at the corrugated tin roof, ripping a corner free. As it flapped and banged, the girls cowered in fright. The lantern, flickering and sputtering in the gusts whipping through

TYPHOON!

the hall, cast shadows that danced eerily across the wall until the wind finally snuffed the flame out, leaving the girls in total darkness.

Kara prayed frantically. A crash vibrated the house. Any second she expected the entire Pacific Ocean to come crashing down on their heads. What if there were a tidal wave? Had God sent them clear across the ocean only to let them be washed away by a storm?

Once again she was the little girl hiding in fear, huddled in the bottom of a closet.

And still the wind howled like demons and the rain thundered like a locomotive charging down on them.

The Christmas Ride

---------- 9 ----------

Kara woke with a start. At first puzzled at finding herself in a cramped position on the floor, she allowed the cobwebs to clear from her mind. Then the memory of the storm hit her. Anxiously she strained to hear the thundering rain, the screaming winds, the pounding surf. But only silence greeted her.

She shook Lynn awake. Together they tiptoed silently down the hall where the gray world greeted them through louvered windows. Absentmindedly Kara pushed several loose louvers back into their slots to keep them from falling to the floor.

As if in a trance the two stood staring at the gloomy scene before them. Palm trees, once proud monarchs of the jungle, slumped over the plucked fronds that lay strewn from one end of the compound to the other. Torn leaves, smashed breadfruit, fallen coconuts, boards, and several pieces of tin roofing littered the disheveled compound. Nature wept as rain dripped from wounded trees.

A pickup ambling slowly toward the mission house caught the girls' attention. They went outside. Lurching to a stop, Mike poked his head out and asked them how they had fared during the storm.

"OK, but what about the rest of the island?" Kara asked. "Is there much damage?"

THE CHRISTMAS RIDE

"Some. Broken trees, torn roofing, battered shacks. But haven't heard about anyone getting hurt. Guess the major part of the typhoon went around us. We were on the outer edge. Praise the Lord! Back 20 years ago a typhoon swept through these parts and washed over a 100 people away."

When Pastor Allen and his family arrived they listened in disbelief as the girls recounted their encounter with the tail of a typhoon. In no time Allen had the generator fixed. Both Kara and Lynn felt relieved to turn the responsibility of the mission back into his capable hands. Now they could be free to enjoy what remained of their Christmas vacation.

Christmas morning burst forth with dazzling sunshine and typical tropical warmth. Sunbeams flashed from one glossy leaf to another. After the brush with the typhoon the island hadn't taken long to recover. Once again the magnificent palm trees stretched heavenward just as proudly as they had before the storm.

The girls went swimming in the lagoon. Kara wondered if Paul had by now opened her Christmas present to him. She had sent him a shell lei with little love notes hooked between the shells on the medallion. There was a note for each of the remaining months they would be apart. Lynn had told her the idea was romantic, but that she didn't envy Kara being away from her boyfriend for such a long time. At last the two girls decided to head back in order to help with dinner preparations.

Kara offered to finish making the breadfruit salad. While she chopped baked breadfruit, eggs, pickles, and onions to be mixed with mayonnaise and salt, Lynn set the table and made fresh lime juice. Just as Jan took a

KARA

casserole from the oven, Allen returned from his trip into town to pick up Ronn.

Mouths watered as everyone gathered around the table laden with horded delicacies saved solely for such a special occasion. Breadfruit salad, candied sweet potatoes, bread dressing cradled between imported vegetarian choplets, steaming rice smothered in rich egg gravy, lime juice served in crystal stemware. Kara eyed the bowl containing olives and pickles. She hadn't seen an olive in four months. Two thick pumpkin pies sat on a nearby shelf.

With mixed feelings Kara glanced about the table. A sudden wave of homesickness swept through her, but not for long, for as she spotted Lynn's happy smile and heard Ronn's hearty laugh, the old familiar faces faded into these new ones.

Sitting between the girls as he usually did, Ronn slipped an arm around each of them after Allen's heartfelt prayer. Grinning, Ronn declared, "I sure am lucky to have found such nice friends on this island. Made my stay worthwhile!"

Allen chuckled as he took a serving of salad. "Better enjoy being the girls' center of attention while you can."

Ronn took an olive and popped it into his mouth. "What do you mean?"

The missionary pulled out a letter from his pocket and waved it in the air. "Our third student missionary will be arriving in about three weeks."

"Three weeks!" Lynn squealed "Who is she?"

Allen's eyes twinkled with merriment as he laughed. "She? Ha! Maybe you should try *he*. You're in for some competition now, Ronn."

THE CHRISTMAS RIDE

Ronn choked on his olive while Kara exploded, "That's wonderful! That's the best Christmas present. Help at last!"

Jan tucked a napkin around her daughter's neck. "Now I'll have three extra to feed. When we accepted this call nobody told us we'd be responsible for feeding student missionaries." She sighed. "I guess we'll have to fix the storeroom by the car porch for him."

The girls excitedly looked forward to Tom's arrival, but not Ronn. He fussed and fumed and worried himself almost into a frenzy. Kara noticed and chided him for beginning to act like she had upon his arrival. That seemed to bring him to his senses and he laughed heartily. "I stand corrected!" But lowering his voice he warned the girls to watch out lest the new guy try to take advantage of them. With a chuckle he suggested sending the new guy on a snipe hunt to look for gecko eggs so that he would get lost in the jungle.

Kara shook her head. "Was I that bad?"

Lynn nodded, "You were worse, dearie!"

When it was time for Ronn to return to the village, Allen allowed the girls to drive him back in the mission pickup. "That's a first," Lynn commented as she climbed in beside Ronn who started the vehicle and headed down the long driveway.

Partway to town the group met up with a slow moving car. Ronn tried to pass, but as he did so the beat-up jalopy sped forward. It wasn't long before the vehicle again slowed to a crawl. However each time Ronn tried to get around it, the old car would lurch forward, weaving back and forth across the road.

"Must be some drunks," Ronn muttered. As he attempted to pass once more the old car swerved into their lane. Lynn screamed. Ronn whipped the steering wheel far to the left to avoid a collision. They bumped over huge potholes, barely missing a cluster of towering palm trees. "That guy's not only drunk—he's crazy!" Ronn frowned as he steered the pickup back onto the road.

In a short time they again caught up with the drunks. Once more they careened over into the passing lane. This time Ronn was prepared. Quickly he pulled back to the other side. Driving out onto the shoulder of the road he sped past the drunks. The girls clutched the seat as the pickup lurched forward, speeding down the road until they came to an abrupt halt in front of Ronn's apartment building.

Just as he opened his door squealing tires pulled up beside them. Ronn and Lynn exchanged worried looks.

Leaning from his window, the grizzled drunkard shook his fist menacingly. Curses rolled from his tongue. Lynn shrank back in the seat, her eyes wild with fear. Kara noticed the blood veins rippling across the man's face. She froze as he yelled, "You Seven day people come and try to teach islander and then you do shuch terrible thing as pash me on wrong shide of thish road!" His foul language ripped through the once peaceful night.

"But you . . ."

"You bad people! You break law!"

"But . . ."

The drunkard's curses drowned out Ronn's explanations. Lynn clutched the younger man's arm in fright. Although she appeared calm on the surface, Kara trembled inside. The nightmares of her childhood had come back to life.

THE CHRISTMAS RIDE

The second drunkard staggered over and leaned in Kara's open window. She recoiled from the touch of his hand on her arm. The smell of beer on his breath was all too familiar, and she shivered uncontrollably.

Just then a police car drove up.

"Polish offisher," the burly drunkard announced, "These people break the law. He pash on the wrong shide of the road. Arresht them!"

"Is these true?" the policeman demanded. "Did you pass on the wrong side of the road?"

"Yes, I did, I had . . ."

"Then I will have to arrest you."

"Now just one minute!" Ronn exclaimed. "I'll go to the station with you, but I insist on seeing the chief of police."

Within minutes everybody was at the police station. To Ronn's dismay he found that the chief of police had gone out and nobody knew when he would return.

Ronn and the girls sat down in the hall. The drunks sprawled on the floor and soon passed out. The minutes ticked by slowly. One hour. Two hours. And still the chief of police did not come.

The White Foreigner

10

At long last the official arrived. It took only minutes for Ronn to explain what had happened. Sharply rebuking the police officer, the Chief fined the two alcoholics for drunk driving and harassment of citizens, and told Ronn and the girls that they could go.

Though Christmas break helped revive lagging spirits it also meant the end of the monsoon season. The daily rain clouds vanished. The tropical sun now bathed the island with unrelenting heat.

The mosquitoes appeared to be the only inhabitants who didn't seem to notice that the water supply had dwindled. Their numbers actually increased. And without the monsoons, scarcely a breeze blew through the sweltering classrooms to carry away the pesky insects.

Not to be outdone by nature's pests, the students acted as if they had a contest going to see who could win the grand prize for obnoxiousness. Kara was sure that they spent their nights dreaming up more tomfoolery.

One sweltering afternoon Colonel employed his reading time drawing pictures of famed Karate champions, labeling them "Tomfooler of the Island." Instead of reading his social studies assignment, Kendall used

THE WHITE FOREIGNER

his book for a pillow. Rila sat in her chair calmly braiding her long black hair.

Rip . . . rrrriiiipppp! Kara turned in time to see pieces of torn paper fluttering to the floor beneath Marianne's desk. Kendall wasn't the only hot-tempered student. Marianne had little patience and could fly into an instant rage. When her patience gave out she'd wad her papers up and throw them on the floor, her book and pencil quickly following. As long as Kara reacted patiently to Marianne's quick temper the girl would soon melt into smiles. But if she lost her temper the girl would be as impassable as a turtle in his shell.

One thing Kara could always count on though. Sooner or later Marianne would come to her and apologize. Then once again she'd be friendly. As Kara coped with the tensions erupting in the classroom she awaited the new student missionary's arrival not unlike the imprisoned soldiers awaiting General McArthur's return to the Philippines. She knew that as soon as she had fewer students in the room discipline wouldn't be such a problem.

Kara liked Tom from the first. Tall and slender, with curly blond hair, he impressed her greatly. The son of missionary parents, he took to mission life like a coconut crab to coconuts.

The first morning he shot a few baskets before school. Some of the little boys rushed to join him, but Kara observed with some surprise that the older boys stood aloof to the side. Approaching them, she overheard Nelson say, "Look at that ribele (white foreigner). He one skinny boy."

Miles simply shook his head in amazement. "White skin, white hair. White shirt. Too much white."

KARA

Trying to hide her amusement she suggested that they go play with him.

"I no playing ball with ribele," Miles muttered.

"What? You play ball with me and I'm a ribele."

"You no ribele. You one ru-Marshall."

"Yeah," Nelson agreed. "You like drinking coconut like ru-Marshall, you like many rice, you say many time to me these island like your home." He nodded emphatically, "You one ru-Marshall."

A lump rose in her throat. Always she'd felt like a foreigner. Now they included her as one with them.

Tom took over the middle grades, leaving Kara with only her seventh and eighth graders. To her delight she found that discipline problems greatly decreased. With fewer distractions the students progressed more rapidly and thoroughly through their subjects. But some things did not change. Colonel continued to come without a pencil. Kendall absented himself with the claim that he had "great sickness." Marianne still lost her temper. Classroom artists, Colonel in particular, kept on drawing legendary heroes such as Bruce Lee and Tomfooler. The girls never lost their giggles nor Miles his charming ways.

After school Tom and Kara went for a walk along the beach that he had not seen as yet. He spoke enthusiastically of starting Branch Sabbath Schools, of visiting people in their homes, of learning the language . . .

Kara smiled to herself at his enthusiasm. But she asked him when he would have time for school if he attempted all his projects. "What's a mission for if it's not to do all these things?" he answered. "Perhaps we concentrate so much on teaching reading, writing, and

THE WHITE FOREIGNER

arithmetic that we lose sight of our main goal."

"And what's that?"

"I believe our goal should be to teach them things that will help them cope with the modern civilization their island has been thrust into contact with. Knowing the capital of Spain probably won't do them much good as they make their living fishing or harvesting coconuts. As a missionary I think our purpose should be to instill the love of Jesus in their hearts that they might live upright and useful lives on their small island."

Later that evening Kara and the other teachers were busily working at school. Allen now left the electricity on for a certain amount of time each evening. Suddenly strange sounds from outside startled her.

Quavering, eerie voices rose and fell in the darkness. Somehow she knew it was Colonel and Miles. When they entered her room at last she accused them of trying to scare her.

"We not trying scare you, Karanae," Colonel protested.

The noise returned.

Miles leaned closely and whispered, "Maybe it is the one we call Tomfooler who make these noise!"

After a few minutes Colonel asked nonchalantly, "You like see one tall, very skinny man ride one small bike?"

"Tom?"

Colonel nodded. Kara trooped outside after the boys. Nelson leaped out of the darkness in front of her and she screamed. Tom raced from his room to her rescue.

She laughed. "Nelson you shouldn't scare me like that!"

KARA

The short boy grinned. "Tomfooler he make me do these thing."

Tom raised questioning eyebrows. "Who's this Tomfooler? I haven't met him yet."

Kara laughed until she had to cry. At last she managed to explain who Tomfooler was. As she finished Colonel dragged out a beat up old bike. Good-natured Tom agreed to take a ride. Grasping the crooked handlebars, he careened the wobbly bike down the sidewalk. Without warning it collapsed, spilling him on the ground.

With a gasp Kara rushed to his aid.

"Oh!" Colonel exclaimed. "Are you break your leg?"

Tom slumped to the ground, moaning as if in deep pain. "Get the pastor!" she ordered. "He's hurt! Quick!"

The smirks left the boys' faces. Colonel, biting his fist, nervously mumbled, "Oh, Karanae, I not mean hurt Tom. We only play small trick. We . . ."

"Not now, Colonel. Get help! Now!"

The boy fled toward the mission house.

Troubles

11

As Colonel fled to the mission house, Tom burst into laughter. Kara's mouth dropped open in astonishment. "You aren't hurt?"

He shook his head as he continued to laugh. "The joke's on him now!"

"Joke? What joke?"

"The bike. Half the pieces are missing. I'm sure they did it on purpose so this would happen." Tom wiped tears of laughter from his eyes. "So I thought I'd play a trick on them."

Nelson shook his head in wonder. "You one very smart ribele."

Just then Allen appeared with Colonel lagging behind. "I thought you said Tom was hurt." Turning, he left abruptly.

Colonel's eyes widened with surprise as he stared dumfounded at the new teacher.

Tom rose to his feet and dusted his pants. Sauntering up to the boy, he threw an arm around his shoulders. "Hey! That was some ride. Now it's your turn, that is, after we replace a few parts."

Colonel grinned sheepishly. "You one crazy ribele. Let's go!"

Turning to wave at Kara, Tom said, "Sorry to desert you like this. But I know you have schoolwork to do.

KARA

And me and the boys, well, we've got a bike to fix. Come on guys!"

Colonel grinned from ear to ear. "You one funny man."

Nelson whispered to her before he too left, "I like that skinny boy. I am glad he come to our small island."

Kara agreed with a smile, "Me, too, Nelson. Me, too!"

Tom's enthusiasm brought new life to the mission. His arrival triggered many changes, the most drastic of which involved the school. A lighter work-load made teaching far less tedious and time consuming. Discipline problems decreased. Less schoolwork released more time for other things.

The girls helped Tom hold Branch Sabbath Schools throughout the island. The children eagerly crowded about to hear and see him pantomime Bible stories. Kara, also an avid storyteller, carried her small accordion slung across her back as she went from place to place to accompany the singing that Lynn usually led. Sometimes one of Kara's older students tagged along to act as a translator.

One time she spotted Thompson watching from a distance. Her heart ached for the troubled boy. Gathering a bit of courage she introduced Tom to him. A stranger to no one, the new teacher clapped the boy on the back like a long lost friend. For a moment Thompson's aloofness disappeared. Inviting the boy to return next week, Tom and Kara started to leave, but Tom turned back. "Hey, Thompson. Tomorrow the boys are taking me fishing so I can see how it's done here on the islands. Want to come?"

TROUBLES

The boy answered by raising his eyebrows briefly, then his eyes lit up.

A lump rose in Kara's throat. Quietly she told Tom as they continued their way down the jungle path leading away from the cluster of shacks, "If only you had been here his story might have turned out differently."

"One never knows. I might not have handled the situation any better." He stopped, cocked his head at Kara, and stated optimistically, "Besides, his story isn't over yet!"

Only three of Kara's students were Seventh-day Adventists. Often some of the others had wondered why her church kept Saturday holy instead of Sunday. So one morning she tackled the subject, never dreaming the stir it would cause. When she had finished the students felt sure that some text in the Bible must say that one should worship on Sunday. Kara offered to give $100 to anyone who found it. She urged them to ask their parents, friends, and even their pastors for help.

That evening—Kara learned later—Miles waited for the right moment to talk to his father who was an elder in their church. "Father, why does our church keep Sunday holy?"

"Because that is what the Bible tell us to do."

The boy sighed in relief. "Where does it say that in the Bible?"

Instantly the man sat up straight. His smile vanished and his face hardened. Dark eyes blazed with anger as he spoke through clenched teeth, "Why do you ask this, my boy?"

"Today Kara shows us many text in the Bible saying

KARA

that we should keep Saturday holy and not Sunday. She said. . . ."

His father leaped to his feet. Blood vessels swelled across his thick neck. "She lies! Those Seven day people are wrong! Wrong! Don't believe what she tell you. She only want you to become one of *them!*" The enraged man turned on his wife, "See what happens! I tell you many time not to send our children to that Seven day school."

"But, father," his son pleaded, "I read those text myself. Let me . . ."

With a sweep of the hand Miles' father knocked the Bible from the surprised boy's hand. "This is enough foolishness! Do you think I lie? That our church lie?"

Miles backed away from the angry man. He frowned as his father declared, "Kara is to teach you to speak English. I, your father, will teach you what you should know about the Bible. Don't believe all what Kara tell you. Be wise. Do not bring shame to this house by believing her lies."

The next day Miles went to school with a great sense of disappointment. Kara had lied to him and he had thought she was very wise. Now he fought to keep back the tears that threatened to spill down his brown cheeks. In all his sixteen years he had never felt so hurt.

The minute the students stepped into the room Kara sensed something was wrong. After worship she asked about a Sunday text, only to be greeted by silence. At last Miles muttered bravely, "You lie!"

Other students nodded their heads in approval of his statement.

"No, I didn't lie," she replied softly. "You read the

TROUBLES

texts in the Bible. The Bible is our only true guide. Sometimes men can be wrong." Then she dropped the subject.

Miles' attitude distressed her. Throughout the day he remained sullen and aloof. Never before had he acted that way. When he finally wadded up his math paper and threw his book on the floor she called him from the room, praying as she did so.

"Miles, what is wrong? You've never acted like this."

He bowed his head and remained silent.

"Miles, I'm your teacher but I'm also your friend. If some . . ."

"You tell me one thing and my father he tell me other thing," he blurted. "He say you lie!"

So, the problem was the Sabbath. "Miles," she started softly, "Study the Bible for yourself. It is there that you will find the truth. Pray about it, and I will pray for you. God loves you very much. He will help you. And I'm here if you need me. Why don't we pray about it, now?"

The boy smiled weakly as he glanced into her face. To his surprise he saw her eyes filled with tears.

That Friday night Kara took a walk and sank at last beneath a spreading breadfruit tree, discouragement about to overwhelm her. Feeling totally alone she stared up at the stars. Waves of homesickness flooded over her. When Lynn joined her they began exchanging tales of their hectic week. As the minutes passed each became gloomier and more depressed.

Then a voice behind them broke into their misery. "Did I hear someone mention my name?" Tom plopped down opposite the girls and chewed on a blade of grass.

"I was just saying that things have improved since you came."

He chuckled. "Not sure Ronn would agree with that."

Lynn blushed, having been teased about him all too often.

"We want to go home, Tom. We aren't doing any good here anyway."

"Must be doing some good," he said with a shake of the head. "Satan doesn't bother us if things are going his way."

After listening to the girls vent their discouragements, he reminded them that God had promised in the book of Isaiah that His word would not return to Him without results, so their efforts wouldn't be wasted. "It just might be that another student missionary will see the fruits of your efforts," he told them. With a smile he added, "You might be surprised at who you find in the kingdom of heaven because of something you said or did here on this tiny little atoll."

The hour grew late as the three continued their discussion. After sharing some of her feelings, Kara ended by saying that she felt the Lord hadn't been answering her pleas for help, especially at the beginning of the year when things were so rough.

"Did you ever stop to think that God did send you aid in the form of Ronn?"

Her eyes widened. "What do you mean?"

"You said yourself how helpful he's been, how much advice he's given that has paid off." Then his sense of humor got the best of him. "Why, look at me! The good Lord decided Ronn couldn't handle the job alone so He sent me, too!"

TROUBLES

"Truly the Lord works in mysterious ways!" Lynn teased.

During the church service the following day Kara played her accordion half-heartedly. She tried to content herself with sowing and leave the reaping to another, but it was hard. Suddenly she lost her fingering and her heart skipped a beat. Miles had slipped in through the door along with Nelson. As he took a seat he flashed her a wide smile and entered into the singing. Kara felt her heart would burst for joy.

Later that day Ronn invited the three teachers to come to his apartment Wednesday night for—as he put it—a special deluxe supper. Tickled, Lynn accepted for all of them. Tom and Kara exchanged amused looks. As Wednesday drew closer Kara wondered how they would get to his place on a distant part of the island. Lynn assured her that she'd heard that a bus was now running back and forth from one end of the island to the other. But though Wednesday came the bus never did.

The trio waited for close to an hour beside the road. At last Marianne appeared and offered to flag down a ride for them. A car with two Koreans stopped. At first reluctant to go with them, Kara agreed at last only because Tom was along. She had never hitchhiked before and didn't want to do so now. Tom tried to converse with the Koreans but it was obvious that they could not speak a word of English.

Ronn was quite annoyed to find they had hitchhiked into town instead of using the mission pickup. Lynn reminded him that they'd been allowed to use it only once before. Frowning, he informed them that the bus service was totally unreliable and that it was likely

KARA

that there would be none traveling that night.

Kara moaned while Tom grumbled that they should have stayed home in the first place and gone snorkeling. Lynn frowned darkly at that statement. To avert an argument Ronn invited everyone to the table. To their delight he had prepared pizza. It disappeared all too quickly.

At last they decided they had better start heading back. The three teachers stood forlornly beside the deserted road. Already Kara's feet ached as she thought of the thirty-mile walk before them. Wondering if they would make it back it time for school, she could imagine Colonel quipping, "What! Karanae is play hooky! Not good. Not good!"

Tom tried to cheer them up. Bowing grandly, he said with a flourish, "After you, my ladies!"

Taking a deep breath, Lynn put one foot in front of the other as she started down the blacktop road that disappeared in the darkness ahead. Kara followed reluctantly. Tom loped along whistling a tune.

The Argument

12

After about a mile down the road, the three student missionaries paused for a rest. Though night had long fallen the air still felt warm. The road had been deserted and the whole island had gone to sleep. Dying red embers marked the sites of the evening fires. The only movement and sound came from the ever present mosquitoes. Kara swatted at them right and left.

"We're going to have to keep moving," Tom said as he, too, fought them off.

"I'm not even ready for school tomorrow," Kara sighed.

"No doubt we'll get a sound lecture from Jan," Tom added, "being she feels so responsible for us as she reminds us *so* often."

"Ugh, I don't know if I would have wanted to come if I had known there'd be no bus and we'd get stranded."

"Told you we should have gone snorkeling," Tom stated.

Glaring at him, Lynn snapped, "I suppose you think this is *all my* fault. Seems to me you enjoyed the pizza plenty. You shoveled enough in."

Kara tried to avert a needless argument. "Hey, we're all tired. Let's just save our energy for walking. There's

KARA

. . ." Her voice broke as bright headlights appeared from behind. A car slowed down, passed, stopped, and backed up.

"Want one ride?" a deep voice asked from within.

Kara squinted into the dark interior. She could see a man, a woman, and two small children.

"Yep! Sure could!" Tom answered. Opening the back door he climbed in after the girls.

"We driving to airport," the man stated.

"That would sure help us out." Tom told him. "We're headed for the end of the island."

"That'll leave us only twenty miles left to go," Kara muttered under her breath.

The man drove on in silence. Even Tom, normally talkative, seemed content to lean back against the seat and rest.

Within a short time the car passed the airport. Pulling up to a booth-type store, the man got out, telling them he would be right back. He returned with several cans of pop in his hands. Handing one to each person, he announced, "I will take you to the end of the island."

"Oh, you needn't go so far out of your way," Tom protested, but the man waved his hand and assured them it was no problem.

A wave of gratitude swept over Kara. Suddenly she relaxed. Soon they would be snug back in their own beds, all because of a kind islander who was willing to go forty miles out of his way in the middle of the night for three foreigners he didn't even know. God had provided again. Kara was beginning to discover that He never let her down the way so many people in her past had.

THE ARGUMENT

Several days later Jan cornered Kara and Tom. "Now remember you, two. *No* more students down at the school in the evenings. They make too much noise and we need our rest. The students should leave after class and not come back until the next morning."

Kara groaned. Now it was clear why Jan had seemed so tight-lipped during supper. She wanted to fall through the floor when she heard Tom's reply. "But what's the harm of their staying around to play a game of volleyball after school?"

"After school they are not our responsibility," the woman snapped.

"Well, I'd rather have the students hanging around the mission than down at the local pool hall or theaters."

Jan stiffened. "We have enough to do without being full-time babysitters."

Tom shrugged, apparently oblivious to her rising anger. Kara cringed in her chair as he said, "Ah, they don't need our supervision to play a little game of ball."

Jan clenched her teeth shut, sucked in a deep breath, and spit the words out. "That's the way it is. *You* don't make the rules! *We* do!" Turning she stormed from the room. Heading down the hallway, she slammed her bedroom door behind her.

Scowling, Allen followed after.

Tom glanced at Kara. "I didn't think what I said would upset her so much."

"She doesn't like to be crossed. She's jumped on my case several times, but since I never say anything back, she's not used to someone doing that." Kara started gathering the dishes and carrying them to the sink. "I don't think she's very happy here."

KARA

"Let's say we do the dishes for her," Tom suggested as he helped clear the table. Loud voices issued from the bedroom. The two couldn't help but overhear what the couple said. Kara cringed at Jan's loud, sharp voice. Her hands began to tremble as she picked up the dishes. The fighting. The yelling. It was all too familiar.

"You shouldn't let him talk back like that to me!"

"I don't think he was trying to be belligerent . . ."

Jan burst into sobs, "I feel so frustrated! I can't handle this anymore! We never have any privacy! I spend *all* my time in the kitchen. We're totally responsible for those three overgrown kids who think they know it all. Like the other night. They came waltzing in after midnight. I was worried sick that something had happened to them." She broke into more sobs.

"You don't understand!" Jan responded to Allen's muffled reply. "I feel totally responsible for them. What if something should happen? What if they got sick? Or drowned? We'd be responsible!"

Her husband tried to soothe her. "The year is almost over. Just hang in there. Maybe next year we can make different arrangements."

"Like what?"

Kara and Tom perked up their ears.

"Oh, I don't know. Maybe the student missionaries could have their own apartment where they'd do their own cooking. That would be far less work for you and give us more privacy."

"Promise?"

"We'll work it out somehow."

As the voices grew quieter the words became too muffled to understand. Kara poured the hot water she'd heated in a kettle into the sink and began

THE ARGUMENT

washing. Tom stood by with a towel.

"Guess I can see her point and all," he whispered. "Sometimes we do get a little noisy in the evenings down at the school. Maybe if we'd try to help her out a little more in the kitchen she'd feel better, too."

After a few minutes Tom paused and grinned. "I think I've come up with the solution to the problem concerning the students. If they can't come to us here at the mission—let's take the mission to them! We could quit working at the school earlier in the evenings and go visiting."

"Great idea!" Kara told him as she mopped up the sink area.

Throwing the towel over the empty dish drainer, Tom said with a knightly flourish, "Ready, my Dish Queen?"

Kara giggled. "Yes, O Mighty King of the Dish Wipers!"

Giggling quietly the two left a spotless kitchen and struck off across the compound. Myriads of stars twinkled their approval. For the next couple hours Tom and Kara visited different students in their homes. And at each home it seemed that supper was in progress. Since it was a Marshallese custom to eat when everyone else ate, the student missionaries ended up being thoroughly stuffed. And the islanders were pleased to have them visit in their humble homes.

The Sign of Mourning

13

The days now passed all too rapidly. In two months the girls would be homeward bound though Tom planned to stay throughout the summer.

One afternoon after classes everybody hopped into the mission truck for a trip into town. Palm trees zipped past the windows. The fishy sea breeze cooled Kara as it whipped through her hair. Small groups of pigs wandering about the road ran squealing into the jungle as the pickup roared toward them.

Frosty whitecaps splashed and danced across the oceanside beach seen between the palm trees. Fairy Terns soared high above the treetops. Wispy cirrus clouds clung to the ever azure sky.

The streets in the village teemed with people. Old women strolled leisurely along the sidewalks. Men stood about in clusters. Small boys hung about the billboards, eyeing the movie advertisements of Karate champions. Naked little children darted between the unpainted shanties. Dogs raced about barking loudly.

When Allen returned with the mail Kara was surprised to receive none. "I haven't heard from Paul in two whole weeks!"

Lynn smiled encouragingly as she perused her letter from home. "Maybe he's just busy. Studying for

THE SIGN OF MOURNING

exams." She put her letter down and turned to Tom. "I remember when Kara would get two or three letters from Paul in one week. Once she got five."

Tom chuckled. "Maybe he's suffering from writer's cramp."

Jan poked her head in the back of the truck. "I told you this would happen. Probably found himself a new girlfriend."

Controlling the tremor in her voice, Kara answered, "No, I don't think so. Something else must be wrong."

"You shouldn't always tell her that," Lynn protested. "You only upset her."

Jan shrugged and pushed her glasses higher up on her nose. "Well, she just as well prepare herself for the inevitable." The woman disappeared around the tailgate.

"Never mind her," Lynn said. "I'm sure you'll hear from him soon."

As the pickup lurched down the road Kara did some serious thinking. Maybe Jan's prediction would come true. Her thoughts flew back to others who had gone as student missionaries. She remembered Carla. Before leaving for Japan she had gotten engaged, but when she returned from her year overseas, she and her fiancé had called the wedding off. Kara frowned. Might that happen to her, too?

As they pulled up to a bakery, Ronn rushed up to greet them. He invited everyone to come over to his apartment because he had some exciting news. Curiosity mounted as he maintained his silence until he had served everyone a glass of pineapple juice mixed with coconut milk. Nobody was prepared for the bombshell he dropped.

KARA

"I just got news that I've been accepted for a position on the island of Ponape in the Caroline Islands. Isn't that great!"

Nobody spoke. Everybody simply stared.

Jan was the first to find her voice. "You're leaving?"

He nodded excitedly. "Yep! Ponape is truly a tropical paradise. It's covered with lush mountainous jungles, crystal clear streams, bubbling waterfalls. It has a massive selection of native fruits. Mangoes, giant-sized avocados, sweet juicy pineapples . . ."

Kara turned away and stared dismally at his shell collection. Hardly listening as he spoke about his new promotion, she couldn't believe he was actually leaving. In a way she felt abandoned. A helpless, lonesome emotion she'd experienced as a little girl time and again, once more flooded through her. "And to think I didn't like him at first."

Lynn's voice was barely audible. "You're really leaving?"

"You'll be leaving yourself in a couple of months," he reminded her. He grinned. "Then you'd be leaving me!"

Tears spilled over as Lynn took her glass to the sink. Quickly she brushed them away.

Suddenly Ronn stood by her side. "We've had some good times haven't we?" he asked as he put his arm around her shoulders.

She nodded. "I'll miss you."

"I'll miss you, too. We'll keep in touch." Turning to everyone, he suggested, "How 'bout a sailboat ride? A friend of mine loaned it to me for the day."

"Now?" Sammy squeaked.

"Now!"

THE SIGN OF MOURNING

Everybody momentarily shelved the thought of his impending departure as they gathered at the lagoon. Several sailboats bobbed in the bay. A large craft with brightly colored sails floated nearby. But Ronn pointed to another, moored further out. Jan's face fell when she saw it. Dull green with discolored markings, it looked worn out.

"First we'll have to hoist the mast and rig the sail. Allen, you and Kara come with me."

Ronn pushed a small green canoe out into the water. In minutes the three climbed into the old green sailboat. Allen assisted him in bolting the mast into place. At Ronn's bidding Kara lugged the sail to him and stood by to be of further assistance. Suddenly a splintering noise shattered the air. Kara glanced up in time to see the tall mast falling toward her. Paralyzed with fear she stood rooted to the spot.

"Look out!" Ronn lunged forward, pushing her out of the way as the mast fell with a thud where she had been standing. The boat rocked wildly.

"That was close!" he whistled as he helped her up.

The men investigated the broken mast. "Rotten. The wood is rotten." Ronn stared out at the lagoon. "Just think if it would have broken out there. We could have been adrift at sea for who knows how long."

Kara shuddered. Already she could imagine the headlines in the Union College *Clocktower*. "Three Student Missionaries Missing at Sea." Bowing her head she offered a prayer of thanks. When she opened her eyes the words of a Bible verse flashed across her memory, "Before they call I will answer."

At last the dreaded day arrived for Ronn's flight to Ponape. It was a somber group that arrived at the

KARA

airport to see their friend off. As Kara spotted him her mouth dropped open. When she nudged Lynn, she, too, stared.

Standing in line to get his ticket, he looked strangely different. He wore long slacks, laced shoes, and a flashy orange shirt *with* sleeves. Kara couldn't remember seeing him in anything other than cut-offs, sleeveless shirts, or swimtrunks.

Ronn tried to keep everybody's spirits up. Turning to Tom he tried to get a smile out of the girls by telling him, "Take good care of these girls. They need a strong hand to keep them in line."

"I'll agree to that!" Allen joked as he approached. "Here comes your plane."

Through misty eyes Lynn watched the plane land and taxi up to a complete stop. Quickly she turned to hide the tears that threatened to spill down her cheeks. Sensing the turmoil that must be going on inside her friend, Kara stood beside her.

Ronn observed everything. He'd tried so hard to put on a cheerful front. "Hey, don't be so long-faced. We can all stay in touch."

Tom's eyes twinkled, "Still have me!"

Lynn turned away. Ronn frowned as he watched her go and stand forlornly beside the wire fence.

"Don't worry about her," Kara said. "She'll be all right."

"I know," he answered hoarsely. "She's got some mighty special friends here." He put his arms around Kara and hugged her good-bye. "Take care of yourself."

Kara nodded miserably. Ronn pressed a small package into her hand. "Just something to remember me by," he whispered. She watched gloomily as he shook

THE SIGN OF MOURNING

hands with the others. Tears slipped down her cheeks as he went to Lynn and gave her a hug. Then he headed for the plane.

Tom stood beside Kara. "Won't be long till you get on that plane and head for home yourself."

Home. Paul. Paul? The old, worried feeling wormed its way into her mind and she wanted to cry more than ever—for Ronn, for Paul, for herself. Yes, she would soon be homeward bound but would Paul be there to meet her?

The jet revved its engines. Slowly it started down the runway. The thunder of the exhaust blocked out every noise and thought in her. Kara slipped up to Lynn.

"I can hardly wait till we're in that plane," the other girl said tearfully.

As the aircraft disappeared into the distance Kara nudged. "Let's see what he gave us." Together they unwrapped their small packages.

Bars of soap.

"What a practical gift!" Tom smiled as he peeked over their shoulders. He didn't notice the tear that slipped down Kara's cheek.

The memory of a funeral she'd attended the first week she had been on the island came back as she gazed at the soap. The mourners who came to the funeral had each brought a bar of soap or a box of detergent. They gave it to the family of the deceased as a sign of their mourning.

"No, Tom, it's more than that." She slipped the bar of soap into the pocket of her dress and headed slowly for the pickup.

Tomfooler Rides Again

14

"What are three types of burns?"

"First, second, and three degree burn," LeGayling answered.

"Booker, describe a first-degree burn . . ."

"Oh, maybe it one very bad burn."

"No, not a bad burn," Kara corrected. "A very bad burn is a third-degree burn. A first-degree burn is mild. The skin is just red. Which type has blisters, Miles?"

"Second-degree."

"What do you do if your clothes catch on fire?"

"Pour gas on him!" Kendall blurted, thinking he had made a great joke. Nobody laughed.

"No. If you did that you would burn the person all up. Marianne, what would you do?"

"Roll on the ground."

Colonel, trying to look horrified, exclaimed, "What! And make dirty my shirt!"

Kara threw her hands up as the whole class burst into laughter. She gave the students their assignments and each head bent to his or her task. Taking a few free moments, she began correcting a stack of papers. When she glanced up from her work she noticed Colonel busily staring at the ceiling. One by one the others joined him until everybody gazed upward.

With a frown Kara wondered what they were all

TOMFOOLER RIDES AGAIN

watching. Soon she, too, glanced up. With that, the students burst into laughter. "What's so funny?"

Colonel wagged his finger at her and slapped his knee with his other hand. Marianne spoke for him, her dark eyes dancing merrily. "He play last joke on you. He make you thinking there is something on ceiling."

Chuckling, Kara told the students to finish their assignment.

Kendall's hand waved back and forth in the air. "I need go to small house."

When Kara gave him permission she failed to notice that Colonel slipped out behind him. Just before lunch Pastor Allen burst angrily into the room. "Who removed the mission sign?"

"What?" Kara asked.

"The sign to the mission. It's gone. Poles and all!"

With a sinking feeling she spotted the all too innocent look on Colonel's face. Kendall, too, acted far too interested in his science book.

"I don't know how you did it or who did it," the pastor continued, " but whoever did it had better return the sign. Immediately!" Whirling around, he stomped angrily from the room.

For a few startled moments Kara stood in front of the room. Were Colonel and Kendall guilty? Even if they were, when could they have done it?

She couldn't help but giggle as she thought of a similar situation in the Bible. "Ok, Samson, you better put the sign back. The pastor is pretty upset."

Colonel looked innocently around him. Leaning toward Miles he asked, "You know this Samson boy?"

Miles shrugged.

Whispering loudly in the direction of his teacher,

KARA

Colonel announced, "I tell you who these Samson is?"

"Who?" Kara prompted.

A smile played about the corners of the boy's mouth as he said, "these Samson—he is one we call Tomfooler!"

She laughed so hard that tears rolled down her cheeks. Before lunch she checked to see if the sign had reappeared. It had. And she arrived just in time to see two forms, unmistakably Colonel and Kendall, slinking into the jungle. At lunch Allen grumbled about wishing he knew who had done it.

"I bet I know who did it!" Tom chuckled.

Kicking him under the table, Kara frowned him into silence.

"But, I really couldn't be sure," he hastened to add.

One day Nelson didn't come to school until the afternoon recess. Spotting him sprawled lazily under a breadfruit tree where he watched a volleyball game, Kara went over to him. "Good to see you, Nelson. I missed you."

"You have many student. You not need me."

"Oh, but I do. Each one of you is very special."

The boy chewed on a lime. "How long you live with your sister?"

"Since I was in sixth grade."

Nelson grinned. "Just like me. I living with my sister now two year."

"Where is your father?"

"I don't know. Maybe on outer island. He not care about me. Why you not live with your parent?"

She paused before answering. How could this island boy understand? "My mother died when I was a small girl. My father got married again but they soon

TOMFOOLER RIDES AGAIN

began drinking too much beer. They would come home drunk all the time, get into big fights, and beat each other. They would break things in the house. Most of the time we had no food. I was hungry all the time."

Nelson nodded knowingly.

"The kids in school would tease me and call me drunkard's daughter. They would say bad things about my father and me." Kara got a faraway look in her eyes as she remembered many things. Shivering, she tried to shove the haunting memories back into her mind's closet.

"When I was 12 my sister and I went to live with our oldest sister. Since then I have lived with her family."

"My dad drink beer all the time too," Nelson said. "Many time he come home and fight me. He hurt my mother many time and she run away one day. I never see her again."

Kara's heart cried in sympathy.

"Sometime when my father come home I go hide. Then he cannot find me. He yell and he yell but I no answer. He fight me bad many time. I much afraid."

As Kara listened it was as if she were hearing someone else tell her own story. She turned away to hide the tears, and in them found relief. In fact the more she and Nelson talked the better she began to feel. It was like being freed from a prison she had made for herself. Trying to keep all the childhood memories locked up had been a losing battle. Talking about them, Kara mused, seemed to release her from their chilling hold.

"My sister say to my father one day that he no good

KARA

and she take me away to her home. But she have many children. She not need me. I wish . . ."

"What?"

"That . . . I have one sister like you," the curly-headed boy blurted.

Kara smiled, at the same time fighting for control of her voice. "Nelson, back in North Dakota there is another boy, just a little older than you, who I call my little brother, even though he really isn't. He calls me his big sister. If you would like, I will be your big sister, too."

Nelson also smiled, his dark eyes shining with delight. "I like that very much. Always I be your little Marshallese brother. And you will not forget me when you go away from these one small island?"

"No, I will never forget my little Marshallese brother." Wistfully she added, "Someday we'll be in heaven where we'll never need to say goodbye. The ocean will not separate friends and loved ones. In heaven the people will be happy. They will not drink beer or hurt each other. Families will be together. No one will be sad or lonely."

"I will like that. I hope Jesus He coming soon."

Marianne remained after school and demurely sat down beside Kara who was correcting papers. The island girl quietly braided her thick hair into one long braid that reached the middle of her back. Shyly she brought from a hidden pocket an exquisitely formed heart-shaped, paper-thin shell. "These shell for you. I sorry I so bad in school today."

Kara reflected on the latest temper tantrum Marianne had had that afternoon. The impatient girl had shredded her math paper, flinging all the pieces and

TOMFOOLER RIDES AGAIN

her textbook across the room. When Kara had picked up the book and placed it back on the desk of the angry girl, Marianne hurled it against the wall a second time. The book knocked a narrow glass louver from its slot and it had fallen to the floor where it shattered.

In exasperation Kara had taken a wooden spoon and tried to spank her on the back of her legs. But she'd hit the chair leg instead, and the wooden spoon had broken in two. Feeling she'd lost control of the situation, Kara had retreated to her desk and ignored the sullen girl. Several minutes later Marianne retrieved her book, cleaned up the glass, and started working on her assignment.

Now here she was. Kara took the shell. Reaching over she gave the girl a tight hug. "Marianne, there is only one thing that can help you keep your temper. Prayer. When you begin to feel angry, pray to Jesus. He will help you." Softly she added, "I, too, am sorry that I lost my temper. Will you forgive me?"

In answer the girl hugged her teacher and whispered, "I am glad you are come to these island. You are very best teacher I ever had."

The stack of papers that needed correcting soon disappeared with Marianne's help.

The end of the year rolled around. As Kara worked on report cards Colonel trooped into the room, Miles and Nelson following close behind.

Peeking out from beneath his floppy black curly hair, Colonel asked, "You making one report card for me?"

"Yes."

"I hope I get many D."

"Colonel! You don't want to get D's!"

KARA

The boy grinned as he told her, "D stand for dollar. I want many dollar. See, I telling my father D is good. So he give me many dollar. C he stand for candy!"

"You know what F stand for?" Nelson asked.

She waited for him to answer his question.

"F stand for flower!" His eyes lit up mischievously as he added, "You F Colonel and he bring you many flower."

"Boys! Boys! Such tomfoolery!" She wondered if Colonel's father did indeed believe such nonsense. Since he spoke no English he very well could.

The group talked quietly for sometime. Kara wanted to keep the noise down so as not to anger Jan. After awhile she channeled the conversation to what the boys wanted to be when they were out of school. Colonel replied, "Oh, I will be one lazy Tomfooler. Sit under tree and strum my ukulele. Drink much coconut all day."

"Oh, be serious!" Kara giggled.

Strutting across the room, Colonel said, "I will be big fisherman. I will catch many tuna."

Nelson decided he would be a copramaker. A copramaker spent long hours gathering coconuts, husking them, breaking them in two, and drying and chipping the coconut from the shells. After that the copra was bagged and shipped to the states where it was made into flaked coconut.

Miles spoke with such determination that Kara felt taken back, "I want to be a preacher just like Paul in the Bible."

After the boys left Kara gazed across the room, thinking about her students. She thought back to all the times when she had been discouraged, lonely,

TOMFOOLER RIDES AGAIN

frustrated, or tired. Then she looked into the future and envisioned Miles, grown up, standing behind the pulpit, spreading the gospel of Christ in a way she could never do. Standing near him was Nelson, guitar in hand, singing his sermon, an honest, upright copra-maker. In a small wooden shack Colonel knelt, his family gathered around him, lifting their hearts in prayer. She smiled as she thought of Marianne as the teacher, or better yet, as the nurse. "Yes, Lord, it's been worth it all—every tear, every pain, and every heartache."

Rising from her desk she headed for the door. Spying the volleyball on the shelf she picked it up in order to put it away. Just as she was about to toss it into the bin she noticed large, bold, black lettering on the side of the white ball, "Tomfooler Rides Again!"

When You Leave He Will Cry

―――――― 15 ――――――

The countdown had started. Only ten days remained until the girls would leave for home. Excitement ran high as the school year neared its closing. Kara had little time to reflect on a recent letter in which a girlfriend back at college had written about seeing Paul studying in the library on several different occasions with a blonde-haired girl. Doggedly Kara attempted to keep her mind on her schoolwork, the eighth-grade state exams, and graduation. She tried to tell herself that there must be some logical excuse, but Jan's words haunted her. And then, too, she hadn't received a letter from Paul in two weeks. It was becoming a habit of late. Could it be that he really had found another girlfriend?

As Kara walked to the mission house for lunch she mused how natural it had become to pray about everything. She often found herself praying about so many things, no matter how big or how small the matter was. God seemed to have come closer to her somehow, or was it the other way around? So many times He'd been there for her, even sending help before she'd asked for it. It felt so wonderful being able to trust Someone so fully. Someone who didn't desert you—like Paul.

Entering the kitchen she joined the others at the

WHEN YOU LEAVE HE WILL CRY

table. Allen held a letter high in the air and exclaimed, "Kara, the wait is over!"

He flipped the letter to her. Catching it, Kara stared at the bold printing so familiar and so loved. The fat letter had required two stamps. Kara hardly dared to think what it might say. With trembling fingers she placed it in the pocket of her dress and picked at her meal.

Finally Lynn nudged her, "You're not eating anyway. Why don't you go read what he has to say."

Excusing herself, Kara made a mad dash to her room. For a full five minutes she held the letter, too frightened to open it. A frantic tear seeped out of her tightly squeezed eyes. Breathing a prayer for strength she tore open the envelope.

But wait! She couldn't read it here. Glancing at her watch she saw that she had half an hour before school started for the afternoon. Flying from the room she raced down the well-worn jungle path, hardly noticing the delicate spider lilies along the way, until she came to the beach where she had spent so many countless hours. Here, where she had received so much inner strength from the Lord, here where the waves crashed thunderously upon the reef, she would find solace in nature's majestic power.

Nervously she unfolded Paul's long overdue letter.

After several moments she squeezed her eyes tightly shut. Two tiny tears trickled down her cheeks. "How could I have doubted you, Paul!" she whispered. He'd been studying for finals and working on several projects at once. Thinking she'd soon be home anyway, he used some of his letter writing time to complete a project for one of his classes. He explained that the

KARA

professor had assigned everyone a partner for the project. "That must be the girl Dena saw," Kara thought in relief. Assuring her of his love, he said he would see her soon.

Kara clasped the letter to her. She knew that it would be well-worn before she was done reading it over and over through the remaining week. Glancing out to sea, she noticed several dolphins playing in the distance. Frothy whitecaps thundered on the outer reef. The waves rolled over and over until they had spent themselves on the beach. She wriggled her toes in the warm water. Two brown booby birds playing a game of chase in the sky caught her attention. She watched until they disappeared behind the coconut palms bending over the restless blue waves. Lifting her face heavenward she breathed a prayer of thankfulness before returning to school.

The day of the eighth-grade state exams arrived. For months Kara had drilled her students in preparation for them. Allen drove Kara and her eighth-graders to the meeting place at the neighboring public school. Nervously her students took their assigned seats. Kara's stomach twisted into knots. Over and over she asked herself if she'd covered everything, if she'd gone over the right material, if she'd prepared them to mark the answers correctly. She could tell from the actions of her students that they were just as anxious as she.

After the tests had been passed out Kara slipped to a position where she could peer over some of the students' shoulders. Then, taking a seat in the back, she relaxed. After the tough test she'd already given her students, this one would be a cinch. Her seventh-graders could easily have passed it. Miles must have

WHEN YOU LEAVE HE WILL CRY

realized how simple the test would be, for he turned and flashed Kara a knowing smile. His previously troubled eyes twinkled brightly once again.

Even the oral drills went well thanks to Ronn's expert advice. The government examiner used some of the exact questions that Ronn had shared with her.

When all the tests had been finished and corrected, she searched the posted results. Every one of her eighth-graders had placed at the top of the list. Despite the difficult discipline problems a lot of learning had gone on. Pride in her students and gratitude to the Lord swelled in her heart as Kara left the testing center.

Preparation for graduation, finishing things up for the end of the year, and last minute details now soaked up every spare moment of the teachers' time. After a particularly trying day the three of them fell exhausted into some classroom chairs after the last student had gone. Beads of perspiration trickled down Tom's face. Lynn swatted aimlessly at a whining mosquito. Spying a small lime, Kara picked it up, peeled one side, and bit into the sour thing. As her mouth puckered, she wondered what the students found so tasty about the fruit.

Suddenly the door banged open and in sauntered Miles and Nelson.

"Wow! Look at these boy!" Miles exclaimed as he pointed at Tom. "He look like one lazy Tomfooler!"

"Why you not looking for one coconut?" Nelson asked.

Tom wagged his finger accusingly at him. "Why should I? You promised to bring me one this time."

A slow grin spread across Nelson's face as he

winked at Miles. "You want coconut. I bring you coconut."

"So much for your coconut," Kara shrugged. "Might be awhile."

Before the words were out of her mouth in stumbled the boys, carrying between them a large, woven, palm frond basket overflowing with coconuts.

Tom's eyes flew open in surprise. He licked his lips as he thanked the boys profusely. Picking up a nut he jabbed one of the little indentations at the end with his pocket knife. Handing one to Kara, he prepared another for Lynn, one for each of the boys, and a final one for himself. Long after the girls had had their fill of coconut milk, Tom and the boys were still drinking, opening one coconut after another.

Holding a nut up high, Tom said with satisfaction, "Perfect way to end the day."

But the day was not over. After Tom and Lynn left, Kara sat visiting with the boys who seemed reluctant to leave. Miles grew quieter with each passing moment. Finally he went to the windows where he stared out into the darkness. Kara, puzzled by his behavior, said nothing, but wondered.

Angrily Miles struck his fist against the bookshelf in front of him. Kara started from her desk but Nelson laid a restraining hand on her arm. "He will be all right. He upset because you go." Quietly he added, "When you leave these boy Miles he will cry."

Tears sprang into her eyes. She understood the turmoil he was going through because she herself, was suffering the same thing.

Miles turned and cast a pitiful look in her direction. The softly spoken words he uttered twisted her heart,

WHEN YOU LEAVE HE WILL CRY

"Don't go back to North Dakota, please don't go back."

Kara opened her mouth to say something, anything, but nothing came. She wanted to say she'd stay for she'd grown to love this island, these people, these students. But she had to return home. Oh, why were goodbyes so hard to say? In a choked voice she vowed, "I'll be back." It was a promise she would keep.

"Come on, Miles," Nelson muttered. "We will going now." Silently they left and melted into the night.

The slight tremor in the boys' voices reminded Kara of how it was to try to talk when all you really wanted to do was cry. She wondered vaguely if she would have applied to be a student missionary had she known it would have been so heart-wrenching. As if searching for the answer she glanced around the deserted classroom. The silence chilled her. Abruptly she stumbled out into the night.

Midnight Swim

16

Kara wandered slowly across the dark mission compound. As she walked aimlessly along she remembered the games, the happy shouts of the children at play; she thought of the good times, and yes, even the bad ones. Wistfully she wondered if her successes would outweigh her failures. And more importantly, had she done all she could to bring her students closer to the Lord?

She sank onto the hard ground. Overhead the stars glittered like diamonds on black velvet. The sea breeze caressed the leaves, rustling them softly, creating the ever present Wind Song of the Island and Sea. The lilting melody had become a familiar tune throughout the year. But now the song taunted her, making her feel a traitor for leaving the island. Caught up in the spell, she almost decided to stay. She knew she could continue on as a volunteer worker. Maybe, she reasoned, it wasn't so important for her to return and get her teaching degree after all. Or was it?

"Oh, what's the matter with me! I *want* to go home! I'm tired of the endless hassle. I've never worked so hard and so long in my life. Boy, was that professor back at college right when he said that the mission field was no glamor trip." His exact words, spoken so gruffly before the group of newly chosen student

MIDNIGHT SWIM

missionaries, still rang in her ears. "If you're expecting an all-expenses paid vacation or a bed of roses, you might just as well stay home." It certainly hadn't been a vacation. Nor had it been a bed of roses. More than once Kara had wanted to pack up and fly home. The hard times had been many. At times the frustrations had been overwhelming.

She glanced at the sky. "I'm glad to be going home, stars! Do you hear me? Glad!" With that she collapsed in tears. Great sobs racked her body. Finally gaining control of herself, she whispered tearfully, "But Lord, I just can't bear the thought of saying goodbye to these kids. We've become like sisters and brothers, and if I leave, I may never see them again."

The Wind Song of the Islands faded to a sad whisper as if sensing the turmoil of her heart and mourned her going. Rising, she walked without a destination. The next thing she knew she stood by the sea, the waves lapping at her feet.

The ocean. Like a magnet it had attracted her. Often she had found solace in its magnificent thundering power. How long she stood there she never knew. For a time she resisted the impulse, but overcome at last, she glided into the warm waters. She laughed. She cried. She splashed. She dived. At last, floating on her back, she gazed at the dome of stars overhead.

"Karanae! Is that you?"

Gasping in embarrassment, Kara found her footing and stood up. Fully clothed, her hair dripping, she knew she must look ridiculous standing waist deep in the lagoon in the middle of the night.

A girl stepped out of the shadows. "You silly teacher! You swim now?"

KARA

Kara smiled in relief. "Come on, Marianne. Join me!"

Marianne needed no urging. With much splashing she raced into the water and glided forward underneath the surface. Kara shrieked as the girl grabbed her legs, pulling her under. For some time the two frolicked in the lagoon like two playful seals.

Later that night Kara fell exhausted into bed. The warm memory of the pact she and Marianne had made still rang in her ears. When Marianne had whispered tearfully how much she would miss Kara, she pointed to the Big Dipper. She told the girl that she could see those same stars in North Dakota. Because of that, each promised that whenever they saw the Big Dipper they would think of the other, and then, they would not seem so far apart.

During the night the voices of her students haunted her dreams, "Tomfooler!" "Be quiet!" "Put the fan by me." "Give me one pencil." "You silly teacher!" "When you leave he will cry." "I want to be a preacher just like Paul." "I will miss you." "Karanae!" "Kara! Kara!"

". . . . Kara! Wake up! It's time for breakfast." Lynn's face appeared hazily in front of her eyes as she tried to focus them. The voice sounded so far away.

"Uh, sleep, I'm sooo tired. . . ." Kara's voice trailed off, then she jerked with a start into a sitting position. "Oh!"

"Yeah, sleepy head, wake up!"

"Breakfast! I'm awake now. Guess I've been dreaming."

Hurriedly she dressed and followed the other girl into the house. Another busy day had begun.

Screeching into the driveway, Pastor Allen brought

MIDNIGHT SWIM

the pickup to a lurching stop. Graduation day had arrived. Everyone was busy doing last minute details. Grabbing some parcels, the pastor rushed into the house, calling loudly for Lynn and Kara.

"What's all the hollering about?" Lynn asked as she entered the porch.

"Look what Ronn sent you two gals—special delivery—for graduation." He held out two boxes containing large corsages of orchids.

Lynn gasped over their beauty and dashed off to show Kara. The corsages added a special touch to the new dresses the girls had each gotten for graduation.

The hour for the ceremony drew near. Kara dashed down to the school to make sure everything was ready. Woven palm fronds hung from the ceiling like streamers. Mounds of freshly strung flower leis waited for the eighth-graders to place them around the necks of the parents.

Eighth-grade graduation for the islanders took on grand proportions since most of the students wouldn't finish high-school. A potluck supper prepared by the parents would follow.

Kara listened proudly, though nervously, as LeGayling and Miles delivered speeches for their class, first in English and then in Marshallese. Several more speeches followed, intermingled with music. After the potluck supper, people began drifting home.

Leaning against the side of the school, Kara sighed. She eyed the table overflowing with basketry and other mementos that the students had given to the teachers to remember them by. She would treasure each one of them. Her thoughts turned to the next day as she began to pick up litter from the ground.

KARA

    D-Day. Departure Day. All that was left to do was last minute packing and the cleaning of the classrooms. It had all come to an end so quickly.
    "Karanae," a soft voice said.
    Kara jumped for she thought she had been alone. Miles came up to her. His tie lay crazily draped over his unbuttoned shirt. He reached out his hand to shake hers.
    "I want to thank you for coming to these island and teaching me many thing." His voice cracked and his dark eyes glimmered with unshed tears. "I will miss you very much when you leave."
    Controlling the tremor in her own voice, Kara answered quietly, "I will miss you, too, Miles."
    Out of the shadows stepped Nelson. In his hands he held an intricately hand-woven, brightly colored basket. Thrusting it into her hands, he mumbled, "Karanae, I will . . ." But he couldn't finish for the lump in his throat choked him. He turned his head and disappeared around the corner to hide his tears.
    Marianne appeared from out of the darkness and put her arms around Kara. "Oh, Karanae, I don't want you to go away from our island."
    The soft strum of a ukulele interrupted the somber group. Colonel's tie hung like a limp snake from his pocket. His feet were once again bare, having escaped their prison of hard-leather, laced shoes purchased solely for graduation. The shaggy-haired boy continued singing as he approached Kara. Then with a flourish he held out a net bag he had hooked onto his belt.
    "These for you."
    Her mouth gaped open. Through the netting she

MIDNIGHT SWIM

could see several shells, tiger cowries, spider conchs, intricately decorated cones. She accepted graciously.

"My mother she cannot make basket like these boy mothers. And when you go to North Dakota I want you not forgetting these Tomfooler boy."

"I could never forget you." Looking around at the others, she added, "Or any of you."

It was long after midnight before Kara and her students unwillingly parted.

The magic of that night still lingered when Jan called her aside the next morning. As she went up to the house her stomach churned into knots. She figured she'd get a tongue lashing for having allowed the students to hang around so late the night before. But then again, maybe she had done something else wrong. She entered the kitchen with trepidation.

Good-bye, Tomfooler, Good-bye

17

Kara waited quietly while Jan finished brushing her little girl's hair. Her nervousness increased with each second.

At last the woman turned to her. "I just want you to know that I hope there's no hard feelings between us. You've been really helpful around here, and I really appreciate it. I'm so sorry that we seemed to be at odds so much of the time. And I'm sorry if I've come across as being overbearing or having expected too much from you."

The girl's mouth dropped open. Her jumbled thoughts finally produced words. "I . . . I'm sorry, too."

"I know a lot of the problem was my fault. I've always been one to talk before I think, and I don't believe I ever gave you much of a chance to open up."

"I . . . I know I have a hard time sharing my feelings, but maybe if I had, we could have gotten along better."

Jan nodded. "I believe you hit the problem. There was a definite breakdown in communication, but it wasn't all your fault." She went to the window and looked out. A wistful expression crossed her face. Shoving a stray lock of hair into place, she admitted, "I've had a hard time adjusting here. Maybe I've been too much like Lot's wife by longing for the convenient way of life I left behind in the States." A hint of

GOOD-BYE, TOMFOOLER, GOOD-BYE

frustration tinged her voice. "You and Lynn get to return home, but I have another five years to go. I envy you that."

Kara wondered what she could say, but Jan continued talking. "Sometimes I don't know how I'll stand it here for another minute." She smiled faintly. "I'm sorry you've gotten the brunt of my frustrations so often. But I know you have things to do. I better start breakfast."

As Kara started out the door, Jan called after her, "I really hope the best for you and Paul."

Kara could only manage a "Thanks." As she headed for the school building she pondered Jan's words, letting their impact soak in. A load seemed lifted from her shoulders. She wished regretfully that she and the woman had taken time to really talk and listen to each other.

Several students came to school that morning to help Tom and her clean up the grounds and rooms. They had just finished when Jan appeared and invited everyone up to the house for breakfast, students included.

"Wonders never cease," Tom whispered as he walked alongside Kara toward the house minutes later.

"Especially when the Lord's at work!" she replied with a grin.

The students trailed behind the teachers, each looking more miserable than the other. Nobody seemed to be very hungry or in a mood to talk. Tom decided that everybody needed some livening up. Sidling up to Kara, he whispered, "This group needs something to cheer them up." His eyes twinkled mischievously. "Can I borrow that new long dress you just made?"

Her brow puckered with a frown. "My long dress? Whatever for?" Noticing his smirk, she went and got it without another word. Tom immediately disappeared with it down the hall.

Minutes later he returned and posed in the doorway like a model in a catalog. For a few stunned moments everyone simply stared at him. Colonel choked on a piece of banana as he gawked at the teacher posing in a brightly flowered muumuu.

Kendall burst into laughter, and the others instantly joined him. The more they laughed the sillier Tom acted and the louder they giggled and hooted with merriment.

"Look at these woman!" Miles shouted.

Finally Kendall managed to collect himself long enough to hoot, "I have new name for you. It is Rosie!"

"Hello, Rosie!" Colonel yelped. "Will you marry me?"

"You!" Kendall protested. "No! She will marry me! I will make her cook my food and wash my dirty shirt and sweep the floor. Let's go Rosie!" Grabbing Tom's elbow, the fuzzy-haired boy tried unsuccessfully to usher "Rosie" from the room.

Speaking in a high squeaky voice from behind a woven fan, Tom said, "Me! Marry you! How preposterous!"

Miles laughed so hard he lost his balance. When he fell against Colonel, both boys spilled onto the floor where they continued to whoop and holler, all the while holding their aching sides.

For a while everyone forgot the impending good-

GOOD-BYE, TOMFOOLER, GOOD-BYE

byes. But the inevitable moment arrived. Tom carried the suitcases to the pickup. Noticing that Nelson had disappeared, Kara turned to Miles and asked where the other boy had gone.

"He crying. He crying because you go."

Kara followed his gaze toward the school. She found Nelson in a miserable heap behind the school.

"Nelson, please come with us," she said softly as she joined him on the ground. "I would miss you if you weren't at the airport to say good-bye."

Nelson turned tearfilled eyes toward his friend and teacher. Grabbing her wrist, he asked almost fearfully, "You will not forget your little brother when you go back to state?"

"Never!"

"I wish you stay here on these island."

Kara swallowed the lump in her throat. "One day I will come back, Nelson. I promise."

The two returned and climbed into the back of the pickup. More and more piled in until Kara and Lynn found themselves buried in a sea of brown faces. Tom, Miles, Colonel, and Nelson perched precariously on the shut tailgate, hanging on for dear life as the loaded pickup lurched down the bumpy road.

Tears filled Kara's eyes as she gazed at the glimpses of the ocean through the palm trees for she knew she was seeing it that way for the last time.

Feeling someone slip their hand into hers, she looked into Marianne's tear-stained face.

"Karanae, you are happy now that you will see Paul?"

Kara smiled. "Yes, but I am sad because I will not see you for a long time."

KARA

More students and friends were already at the airport waiting to see the girls off. One by one they slipped flower and shell leis over Kara and Lynn's shoulders.

Nelson shook Kara's hand gravely and quickly hid his tears.

"Good-bye, little brother. I will see you again. If not here, then in heaven."

The boy nodded. When Miles shook her hand she felt her heart being wrenched from her. The good-byes were just too hard to say. Neither could speak. Seeing Colonel, Kara reached in her pocket and held a pencil out to the boy.

Smirking, Colonel asked mischievously, "Oh, time make school now?"

"You'll need it for high school," she whispered as she choked back the tears.

He shook his head. "I no like high school. Me? I make the copra now." Reaching into his pocket, he took out a folded, worn piece of paper and handed it to her. "Here. These is for you. Tomfooler he say to me 'Give these picture to Karanae.' "

Opening the paper, Kara saw a drawing of Tomfooler stretched out lazily beneath a coconut tree. In his hands he held a ukulele that he strummed with eyes closed. Across the bottom of the picture were the words, "Good-bye, Tomfooler."

Smiling through her tears, Kara turned to hug Marianne, Tayla, and the other girls. When she reached Tom she gave him a quick hug and told him to be sure to take good care of her accordion which he had mastered, as had several students. Taking a small

GOOD-BYE, TOMFOOLER, GOOD-BYE

package from her pocket, she stuffed it into his hand. He raised inquisitive eyes.

"This wouldn't happen to be a bar of soap would it?"

"You'll see!" Walking up the ramp into the aircraft, she turned and waved one last time. The blast of cool air from the aircraft made the girl shiver. Finding a seat next to Lynn, Kara stashed her belongings under the seat and fastened her seatbelt.

The jet revved its engines. The stewardess went over her instructions. Craning her neck, Kara looked at the scene outside the window. As the aircraft began to taxi down the runway she wanted to shout, "Stop the plane and let me off!" but she merely gripped her seat harder as the plane went faster and faster. With a lurch it lifted off. Higher and higher it flew, circling the tiny island until it shrunk into a mere strand of green yarn on the deep blue sea. As the jet banked, the island totally disappeared from sight.

For several minutes the girls remained silent. Then for the first time in twenty-four hours Kara had time to take out and read Paul's last letter. Tears clouded her eyes and dropped onto the paper. "I can hardly wait to meet you at the airport, Kara. It's been a mighty long year without you. Much love, Paul." She closed her eyes.

Many had been the time when she'd worried if Jan's ominous predictions would come true. But no, here was proof that Paul was just as eager to see her as she was to see him. The joy of being reunited with Paul and her family helped lessen the sadness of leaving her island home.

But she did notice something that surprised her greatly. The thought of losing Paul didn't frighten her

KARA

nearly as much as it had when she'd thought about it long before. She now realized that if she and Paul did break up, she would be crushed but not broken. The thought amazed her, for somewhere deep within her she had developed a faith that she'd never experienced prior to coming to this one small island. Just as surely as the tide rolled in and out at its appointed time Kara knew that the Lord would help her through anything, even if it meant losing Paul.

For hadn't He been with her that day in the lagoon when she had thought she would drown? She couldn't help but remember the times when the Lord had helped her without being asked—such as the day the mast toppled over in the sailboat, or the time she'd faced Thompson's gleaming knife. Hadn't He provided three special friends to give her human support and encouragement when she'd needed it most? He'd been there for her even during the times when she'd tried to shoulder burdens solely by herself.

So now, she determined to simply keep trusting the Lord where Paul was concerned, knowing that He would work things out for the best.

As the plane banked gently toward the northeast, tongues of fiery reddish orange leaped across the darkening night sky, making it look as if the globe were on fire.

"I almost feel like I'm deserting them," Lynn murmured, not realizing that she had been talking to deaf ears all along.

Pulled back into the present, Kara agreed. "Yes, I know what you mean. There's a part of me that will be forever tucked away on that tiny island. But Lynn, it's at least comforting to know that another student

GOOD-BYE, TOMFOOLER, GOOD-BYE

missionary will return to pick up the torch where we set it down. And after him, another and another, until at last Jesus comes and takes all of us home with Him."

"I'm so thankful I came here as a student missionary," Lynn sighed.

Kara nodded. "Me, too." The tiny yellow disc of the sun slipped out of sight. The once brilliant sunset melted into a narrow band of flaming red that lined the horizon. She closed her eyes. Two tears seeped between her eyelids as she whispered hoarsely, "Good-bye, Tomfooler, Good-bye."